From ABBA to Mamma Mia!

From **ABBA**®
to Mamma Mia!

text by **Carl Magnus Palm**
photos by **Anders Hanser**

BILLBOARD
BOOKS

This edition first published in Great Britain in 2000 by
Virgin Publishing Ltd
Thames Wharf Studios
Rainville Road
London
W6 9HA

PREMIUM
PUBLISHING

Licensed from Premium Publishing, Stockholm, Sweden
© 1999 Premium Förlag – a division of Internal AB
Photographs wherever not otherwise mentioned © Anders Hanser / Premium Publishing
ABBA is the registered trademark of Universal Music AB

First published in the United States in 2000 by Billboard Books, an imprint of Watson-Guptill Publications,
a division of BPI Communications Inc., at 770 Broadway, New York, NY 10003

Library of Congress Cataloging-in-Publication data for this title can be obtained from the Library of Congress.

Library of Congress Card Number: 00–10 29 58

ISBN 0-8230-8317-9

First US printing 2000

1 2 3 4 5 6 7 9/08 07 06 05 04 03 02 01 00

ART DIRECTOR: Fredrik Söder
EXECUTIVE PRODUCER: Wilhelm Wendt
PRINTED AND BOUND IN ITALY

Foreword

PHOTO SESSIONS CAN BE A ROYAL PAIN in the neck for every pop star. Hour after hour of posing, smiling and changing outfits is a gruelling and thoroughly boring process. When you see a photo session scheduled in your calendar, you think, how the hell can I get out of it: "I was sick the last time, so that won't work again. Maybe my mother is sick this time. Or my dog. God, I'd rather do anything but this." But everyone tells you how important it is, and you drain the bitter cup, reluctantly, in compensation tormenting the poor photographer: "That'll do. They said at our office that we don't need any black and whites this time. Could you please speed it up? I've got to go in a minute."

YOU WERE ONE OF THOSE PHOTOGRAPHERS, Anders, and may God forgive us our sins. Wiser now, we know what an important role all those pictures have played in ABBA's career. Not only the ones in your studio, but those you took on tour, in the recording studio and in many other places. And they continue to play an important role in telling the history of pop. We've really enjoyed Carl Magnus' and your book, and so will our children and grandchildren.

AGNETHA   BJÖRN   BENNY   ANNI-FRID

Contents

Introduction

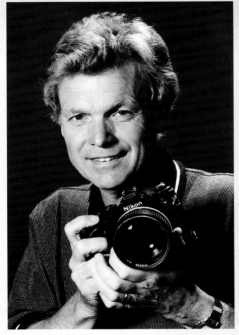

Photographer Anders Hanser has been taking pictures of ABBA and the individual members for over 20 years. Photo by Mikael Bodner, 1999.

THROUGH THE YEARS, countless photographers the world over have taken pictures of ABBA and the four individual members Agnetha Fältskog, Björn Ulvaeus, Benny Andersson and Anni-Frid "Frida" Lyngstad. The group's popularity ensured that wherever they went on their tours and promotional trips, cameras would be constantly clicking and whirring during concerts and press conferences.

The never-ending need for new publicity pictures and photographs to be used on their record releases also meant that ABBA regularly had to show up in the photographer's studio or on other locations for such pictures to be taken. But when the group was actually working in the studio or rehearsing for personal appearances, they would usually prefer to be left alone, which meant that cameras were more or less banned on such occasions.

The result is that during the first five or so years of ABBA's career, most pictures show the group dressed-up and in make-up, all smiles – no doubt genuine ones most of the time – or being mean and moody "rock stars" if that was what was required. Certainly, most of those photos captured the essence of ABBA's public image brilliantly, and many of the best-known and best-loved pictures of ABBA can be found among them.

However, a side-effect may have been that their image as professional posers in some respect contributed to the often-heard description of ABBA as "cold" and "aloof"; perfect pop stars churning out custom-made recordings in their hit factory. Rarely, if ever, was the public allowed a peek at the preparations backstage as opposed to the professionally executed stage show, or at the hard work in the studio instead of the faces on a record cover – "behind the façade", to put it somewhat melodramatically.

ABBA, 17th June, 1981.

Janne Schaffer [top], who played guitar on ABBA's albums, and Polar recording artist Ted Gärdestad [centre] were two of the guests in the TV show **Kika Digga Ding**, hosted by Tommy Körberg [bottom].

At the end of 1978 that situation changed, when photographer Anders Hanser started taking pictures of ABBA. Over the last few years of the group's existence and beyond, he certainly added to the large archive of ABBA publicity pictures, but his lens was also to catch the group members off-guard, working, relaxing – in fact doing all the things we always knew they must be doing, but which they mostly had no reason to show us.

Anders Hanser was fortunate enough not to be regarded as a photographer most of the time. Being the ABBA members' personal friend, and not part of a journalist and photographer team out on a job, his presence went virtually unnoticed, almost without anyone being aware of being photographed. "I think they simply decided not to care that I was there", says Anders himself.

Even so, it was mostly the posed pictures taken in the photographer's studio that reached the general public, and most of those other, more candid pictures were never made into prints. The purpose of this book is to show both sides of ABBA: the professional posers, but also the professional workers.

Anders got the idea for an ABBA book when a couple of the former members celebrated their 50th birthdays in the mid-1990s and he put together some slide show presentations with a "This Is Your Life" theme. "I realised that my archive of ABBA pictures had turned into a kind of treasure chest. All those years ago, it was primarily a matter of taking as many pictures as possible to meet the demand, but with the passage of time all those photographs have acquired a documentary value."

ANDERS HANSER WAS BORN in 1945 in the town of Orsa in Sweden. As a small child he moved to Stockholm, where he has been living ever since. The love for music and images that has been the main thread in his life and career has been with him from an early age.

His parents were both musicians, his mother Hanser Lina Göransson being an opera singer of note. Anders went to music high school in Stockholm, and for a short period in the mid-1960s he played the organ in the pop group Jack Downing & The Other Side. As a photographer he had made his mark even earlier, and already during his teenage years his pictures were published in *Dagens Nyheter* and *Expressen*, two of Sweden's biggest daily papers, as well as in *Se*, the leading photo magazine at that time.

His first professional career was as a teacher, but in 1970 he started working as a producer at Sveriges Radio (Swedish Radio). Around this time, he changed his surname from Göransson to the more unique Hanser, which was his mother's family name. Throughout the 1970s, he was to produce mostly educational and music-related programmes for radio and TV.

It was in connection with one of his TV projects that Anders first made contact with an ABBA member. Producing the music TV programme *Kika Digga*

Ding, hosted by future Chess star Tommy Körberg, Anders asked ABBA to appear in the first show. This was in the spring of 1974, when the group had just won the Swedish selections for the Eurovision Song Contest with "Waterloo".

"I rang Björn up and asked if they would like to appear. He answered, 'Yes, perhaps we might do that, but we want to see how things turn out in Brighton first.' Then, of course, they never appeared on the programme."

However, about a year later the *Kika Digga Ding* team wanted to do a report on how a record was made. The recording session they attended happened to be the one when Swedish singer Harpo recorded his international hit "Moviestar", and one of the backing vocalists on the song was none other than Frida. Anders Hanser took some stills during the session. This was probably the first time that he photographed an ABBA member.

In 1977, Anders Hanser decided to leave Sveriges Radio, and the following year he started his own company, Anders Hanser Produktion AB. However, he continued to produce radio programmes for his former employer under this new umbrella.

What he really wanted to do, however, was to develop projects that combined sounds and pictures into a complete multimedia package, and multislide presentations are what he has mainly been occupied with since. Anders Hanser's clients have primarily been Swedish companies, advertising agencies and museums, resulting in several awards for his work. Many of his productions have also been shown on Swedish television.

The recording session for Harpo's hit "Moviestar", 27th February, 1975. Left: Producer Bengt Palmers and Harpo. Right: Bengt Palmers coaching backing vocalists Lena Ericsson and Anni-Frid Lyngstad.

ACCORDING TO THE MYTHICAL image of ABBA during the 1970s, it was the "cynical" and "cold-hearted" publisher, record company owner and manager Stig Anderson who brought the four group members together. His intention, according to this myth, was that they should then be locked into the recording studio in order to produce hits that would maximise the profits for his company.

In actual fact, when one studies ABBA's story and that of their record company Polar Music, it is remarkable how little cold-hearted calculation it contains. On the contrary, much of their development has been more or less dependent on random meetings, close personal relationships and a kind of family feeling.

Polar and the publishing company Sweden Music were largely built up by Stig and his wife Gudrun, the latter primarily taking care of financial matters, but also acting as a sort of mother figure whom anybody could turn to with their problems. Björn and Benny were best friends who became protégés of Stig and Polar record producer Bengt Bernhag during the late 1960s and early 1970s. Even at this early stage, Stig made a now famous prediction to Björn and Benny: "One day the two of you will write a song that becomes a worldwide smash hit."

When the two boys met Agnetha and Frida in 1969, the four soon became two engaged couples, but they also began a musical collaboration. Agnetha explained in an interview:

"You could say that ABBA was brought together by love. Björn and I were in love with each other, and the same was true of Benny and Anni-Frid. Everybody was in love and we were turned on by each other, not least when we were working together." So it makes sense that it was also love which brought Anders Hanser into ABBA's and Polar's seemingly impenetrable circle of trusted collaborators.

IT ALL STARTED IN THE SPRING of 1978 when Anders was commissioned to produce a series of radio programmes titled *Sommarmorgon* ("Summer Morning"). The theme of the series was that famous Swedish personalities were to talk and play their favourite music in up to five shows each.

Anders wanted the ABBA members as guests in this series, and contacted Polar. The answer came that ABBA wouldn't be available, but that manager and Polar president Stig Anderson would do it. Anders went up to the Polar offices to meet Stig, and there his eyes fell upon 28-year-old Vice President Görel Johnsen. "I had never met her before", remembers Anders. "I thought she was really lovely."

Stig's shows were taped in June 1978, and he and Anders hit it off, both of them being old school teachers. Stig had only positive things to report back to Görel about Anders. In the summer, Polar recording artist Ted Gärdestad taped his programmes for the series. Ted and Anders had worked together several times before and had become close friends. "I asked Ted, 'Is she seeing someone?', and he said, 'No, you should invite her out to lunch', and that's what I did." Soon afterwards the couple were living together, and eventually got married in 1980.

During the summer of 1978, Anders got friendly with ABBA and started socialising with them. At the end of August he took his first photographs of the whole group, purely on his own initiative.

ABBA had been working on what was to become the *Voulez-Vous* album since March 1978. The original intention was that the album should be available in record shops before Christmas, but the sessions were dragging on. There were several reasons, the roots of which can be traced back to the earliest days of the group's career.

ABBA's big breakthrough in Sweden had come in 1973 with the song "Ring Ring". After their victory in the Eurovision Song Contest in Brighton with "Waterloo" the following year, and the ensuing worldwide success, the wheels had started spinning even faster.

In the summer and autumn of 1975 the group's status on the European market had been consolidated with hits like "SOS" and "Mamma Mia", from the album *ABBA*. During 1976 the group had two of their biggest-ever hits with "Fernando" and "Dancing Queen", and this was also when the virtually hysterical ABBA fever in England, Australia and many other countries reached its peak. Despite many promotional trips all over the world during 1976, the group still found time to record their fourth album, *Arrival*, over the course of six months.

1977 was intended to be a calmer year, and after a successful tour of Europe and Australia between January and March, Stig Anderson announced that ABBA would not be available for any interviews or public appearances during the rest of the year, since the group needed time to write songs and record their new album. It had been decided that the album was to be available in the shops before Christmas, so the release would coincide with the première of the feature film *ABBA – The Movie* in December.

Nevertheless, sessions for the album did not begin until the early summer of 1977, and the group soon found that it had suddenly become autumn, and the album was far from finished. Furthermore, Agnetha, heavily pregnant with her son Christian, did not have the strength to work twelve-hour sessions in the recording studio. It seemed unlikely that the album would meet the projected deadline.

The release of the album was provisionally postponed until February 1978, but somehow work was finished sooner than expected, and *ABBA – The Album* was released in the Scandinavian countries a couple of weeks before Christmas 1977.

A selection of ABBA singles featuring photographs by Anders Hanser on the cover.

The year 1978 was already packed with scheduled activities, but after the fast pace of the past few years, the ABBA members tried to at least slow down a little. Despite this, at the end of April and early May a major promotional campaign was to be started in the United States in order to conquer the American market, which thus far had been a little more resistant to ABBA's charms than the rest of the important music markets of the world.

Benny and Stig Anderson visiting Anders and Görel in their home.

In March, work began on the new album, titled *Voulez-Vous* upon its release over a year later. The recording of this album was to take longer, and result in more scrapped songs and difficulties, than any other project.

For example, the first completed track, "Lovelight", was not considered good enough to end up on the album, but was instead relegated to the B-side of the "Chiquitita" single.

And although "Summer Night City" – the last song to be started during the spring – was released as a single later in the year, it is often held up by Björn, Benny and sound engineer Michael Tretow as a recording they're dissatisfied with. Despite the song being slated for inclusion on *Voulez-Vous*, it was decided that it was not up to the standard of the rest of the album.

The main problem for Björn and Benny was finding inspiration; they found themselves in a situation where they could not come up with enough material that felt right for them. Benny later explained: "I suppose this is something that everybody goes through when they have been in the business for as long as we have. All of a sudden you dry up a bit, and then you need fresh impulses in order to get going again."

Björn and Benny complained that these fresh impulses were hardly to be found in the Swedish music climate. Above all, the meagre supply of current English and American pop music on the radio felt like a handicap. "We haven't really got music radio in the way they have in most other countries", remarked Björn. "Of course, you listen to albums a lot, but radio is such a superior medium. Different people select things that they like and then play those songs. Then you can decide if you want to listen or if you want to change to another station, and in that way you get to hear an incredible amount of music."

In mid-May ABBA's own Polar Music Studios were opened in Stockholm, and maybe the fact that they now had access to a place of their own where they could work on their recordings at their own pace made them feel that they didn't really have to use the studio time with maximum efficiency. It is tempting to theorise that Björn and Benny to some extent allowed themselves the luxury of trying out songs in the studio that previously would have been scrapped at the writing stage.

THE FIRST TIME THAT Anders Hanser photographed ABBA was while they were working at Polar Studios – and, typically, during the recording of one of those songs that were to remain unreleased. The backing track for "Just A Notion" was recorded in mid-August 1978, and Anders' pictures show the recording of the vocals, which was probably done a few days later.

Some time later Anders also photographed Björn, Benny and Michael Tretow working at the mixing desk. On this day, they were putting finishing touches to some of the songs they were working on at the time, among them the *Voulez-Vous* track "The King Has Lost His Crown".

As the pictures show, Björn, Benny and Michael would often spend time in the studio doing further overdubs after the backing track and the vocals for a song had been recorded. Michael has pointed out that for Benny in particular there was almost no limit to the number of overdubs that could be made. "Concepts like 'finished' or 'complete' are unknown to Benny – if he had his way, he would work on a song for ever, because he just keeps on coming up with new ideas all the time."

In November 1978, Anders took some photographs at a Rod Stewart concert in Stockholm. Apart from a few pictures he had taken in the early 1960s and intermittently through the rest of the decade – of Fabian, Cliff Richard and Swedish rock king Little Gerhard among others – Anders had never actually been a rock concert photographer.

"The Rod Stewart pictures turned out really well, and I showed them to Görel and to Björn and Benny", remembers Anders. "Through that, and also because they liked my pictures of ABBA in the studio, I was commissioned to do my first official photo assignment by Polar. They were to do a presentation of the Polar Music Studios at the music business convention MIDEM in Cannes in January 1979, so I photographed the studio from all conceivable angles, and of course also ABBA when they were working there."

Both ABBA and Polar liked Anders' photographs, and he was invited to continue taking pictures of them. "I thought that was really important: that they thought that the pictures were good, and that it wasn't just because I was friends with them, although of course that was also an advantage. I could move around freely, and they knew that they could trust me not to release any pictures they weren't happy with."

Thus began a friendship and working relationship that was to continue to

the end of the ABBA period and beyond, through the *Chess* and *Kristina från Duvemåla* musicals, Agnetha's and Frida's solo albums and right up to date with the *B&B* tribute concerts in Sweden and abroad and the new *Mamma Mia!* musical, based on ABBA songs. Indeed, the line was often fairly blurred between an "assignment", and Anders just tagging along to wherever ABBA were going at the time, grabbing the opportunity to take some pictures while he was there.

WHEN THIS BOOK ENTERS the ABBA story, then, the group's most hectic years are behind them. In some respects, they are on the threshold of the final phase of their career. The image of two happily singing couples, who were subjected to an almost hysterical admiration in some countries, is no longer true. Björn's and Agnetha's marriage is falling apart, and during the autumn of 1978 the couple decide to get a divorce. At the same time the explosive interest in the group in countries such as Australia has faded considerably. A few years later, Benny and Frida also break up.

For these reasons, it is a maturing, more grown-up ABBA that is shown in these pictures. The lyrics are beginning to reflect the members' own experiences to a much greater extent, instead of being simply words to carry the melodies. The custom-made, glittery and colourful stage clothes have been thrown away and replaced by high-fashion boutique garments or basic everyday clothes.

It should be noted, however, that ABBA did continue to have major commercial success all over the world during this period – one example is the 1980 album *Super Trouper,* which received record-breaking advance orders of one million copies in England – and it was only during these last years that the group finally conquered the Japanese and South American markets.

This period was also when ABBA's music started being appreciated even by Swedish reviewers, a re-evaluation that during the 1990s has culminated in an almost unreserved celebration for virtually anything that Björn and Benny are involved with, from the major hit musical *Kristina från Duvemåla* to the successful *B&B* concerts of selections from their earliest days as composers up to the present time.

Also included are Agnetha's and Frida's first steps outside the group after the most hectic years – seeking new musical challenges in the shape of solo albums for an international market – as well as *Chess*, Björn's and Benny's first true foray into the world of musical drama.

Benny established himself as a musician and composer with two solo albums released in 1987 and 1989, and his folk music collaboration with the Orsa Spelmän fiddlers. These, together with the 1980s experience of creating

ABBA and engineer Michael B. Tretow during the recording of Just A Notion, Polar Music Studios, August 1978.

a musical, shaped the synthesis that found its ultimate expression in *Kristina från Duvemåla*.

The book ends with pictures from the spring 1999 première of the musical *Mamma Mia!* in London. This final project symbolises the revived interest in ABBA's music in the 1990s and the unbelievable success their music has gained over the world yet again.

IN THIS WAY THE STORY is brought full circle. Simplifying it somewhat, the pictures included in the first few chapters show ABBA's journey towards their break-up. After having had the chance to distance themselves from the most intense ABBA period, and establishing themselves as individual creators of music, all four members have to some extent rediscovered ABBA's music, each in his or her own way.

Both Agnetha and Frida have testified that the 1990s revival has given them the chance to reacquaint themselves with their recorded output. Björn and Benny – particularly the former – have found a way to make their old songs work within the format of musical drama that has become their favoured form of expression.

The former ABBA members have always been proud of what they once achieved as a group, and it certainly looks as if they all now feel safe enough in their current environments – private as well as creative – to let the inescapable ABBA story continue to be a parallel part of their existence.

Björn, Benny and Michael Tretow working on overdubs, Polar Music Studios, September 1978. Benny often wanted to do an unlimited amount of overdubs on ABBA's recordings. "I always had a spare channel, because I knew that Benny would come up with something", says Michael Tretow.

I am your music, I am your song

POLAR MUSIC STUDIOS *December 1978*

ON 18TH MAY, 1978, ABBA'S POLAR Music Studios in Stockholm were inaugurated. The studios had been under construction for over a year, with Björn, Benny and Michael Tretow flying to Los Angeles in the spring of 1977 to check out the technical equipment they wanted. The whole project had originated with Michael Tretow's idea of building a studio of his own. These plans were put on hold for a couple of years when Polar suggested that he should build a studio together with them instead.

The need for studio time was enormous. For ABBA, who spent at least a week on the recording of each and every song, it was frustrating to always have to rent other studios where they were not allowed to work at their own pace for as long as they needed. Their favourite was the Metronome Studio, which was assigned to different record companies on specific days of the week.

Björn, Benny and Michael made a list of everything they wanted to have in the new studio. The idea was that all the technical gadgets and possibilities that were spread out in several different studios now would be available in one single place.

"I remember for example when we were working on some track at a studio called Glen Studio and we needed to get a really good timpani sound", says Michael Tretow. "Well, they didn't have an echo chamber, so when we'd recorded the sound of the timpani we had to go over to the Metronome Studio and record just the echo of the timpani. So what we wanted was a studio where everything was available at the same time."

Among the features of the Polar Music Studios were two 24-track tape recorders, separate rooms with different types of acoustics, open spaces and a lot of glass so that the sound engineer and all the musicians could have eye contact, plus a little mixing console for each musician's headphones so that they would be able to hear the sound level of each instrument as loud as they preferred it.

"The cool thing about the Polar Studio was that we could record strings at the same time as we recorded the loudest trumpets and trombones ever, and still have isolation between them", says Michael.

Agnetha, Björn, guitarist
Lasse Wellander, bassist
Rutger Gunnarsson and
drummer Ola Brunkert
working in the studio.
Sound engineer Michael
B. Tretow at the mixing desk.

"I think the record number of musicians I had there was around 45, all of them playing at the same time, and yet the sound was fully separated. That was just wonderful. The problem before that was that all the different sounds would blend, since studios were built for interaction between the instruments. But when pop music came along, you didn't really want that anymore; you wanted a super-tight sound. On the bass drum channel there should just be bass drum, and so on." Polar naturally wanted to show this well-equipped studio to the world in order to attract international artists, and therefore a presentation was

In 1978, ABBA's Polar Music Studio was one of the biggest and most modern in the world. The studio featured all the technical equipment that ABBA needed to make the recording process as easy and enjoyable as possible.

In early December 1978, ABBA were recording "In The Arms Of Rosalita", a working version of "Chiquitita".

put together for the music business convention MIDEM in Cannes in January 1979. Shortly before the pictures for the presentation were taken, Led Zeppelin became the first foreign star act to use the studio: in November they spent two weeks recording tracks for their *In Through The Out Door* album. Adam Ant, Earth Wind & Fire, Electric Light Orchestra, The Pretenders, Ramones, The Rolling Stones, Genesis and Backstreet Boys are just some of the international pop and rock stars who were later to work on the premises.

ANDERS HANSER'S PICTURES from the Polar Studio were taken in early December 1978, when the group were recording "Chiquitita" – or rather, the song that was to become "Chiquitita". At this stage it was still called "In The Arms Of Rosalita" and was a somewhat slower song that also lacked the characteristic instrumental section at the end. It was only a week later, when the group had found a new arrangement inspired by Simon & Garfunkel's hit version of "El Condor Pasa" and had made a completely new recording, that the song became "Chiquitita".

Today the Polar Studio is still frequently used, even if the demand for studios of its size and scope is not as high as it used to be. The quality of the average recording studio has improved so much during the last twenty years, and studio equipment has become so cheap and easily accessible, that professional-sounding recordings made with synthesizers, drum machines and computers can often be made in very basic circumstances. However, Michael Tretow believes that the natural urge to seek new challenges will bring new life to the more traditional recording studios.

"We have always tried to achieve the impossible. It's no fun trying to achieve the possible. It's no big deal climbing up some small hill, because it's not steep enough and you can't fall down. So I imagine that the generation that has been sitting in garages and doing their recordings will want to try something else sooner or later: 'What happens if we take four trumpets, three saxes and strings, and then record them all at the same time? It must be almost impossible to have control over all that'."

Polar Music Studios in Stockholm

Anders Hanser's pictures of Polar Music Studios were used in a leaflet that advertised the studio.

With a bit of rock music, everything is fine

SURPRISE CONCERT IN LANDSKRONA *18th May, 1979*

GIMME! GIMME! GIMME! *and* ESTOY SOÑANDO

making of promo films, Polar Music Studios, 5th September, 1979

TOUR OF NORTH AMERICA AND EUROPE *13th September – 15th November, 1979*

OVER THE FIFTY-YEAR HISTORY of pop and rock music, extensive touring has remained one of the most important ways for artists to build up and sustain their popularity. The majority of the truly big acts have followed the format "record album, go on tour" very strictly in their careers. Indeed, during rock music's first few decades, right up to the early 1980s, regular touring was an almost obligatory requirement.

Bearing this in mind, and considering ABBA's enormous success and high media profile throughout the ten years they existed, it may seem slightly surprising that the group in fact did comparatively few tours. The only outings that were not limited to Swedish soil were a short tour of Europe during late 1974 and early 1975, a few weeks in Europe and Australia in 1977, plus the 1979 tour of North America and Europe, followed by two concluding weeks in Japan in 1980.

The reason for this limited touring was simply that ABBA preferred working in the studio, and did not want to spend too much time away from their homes and families. Furthermore, all four – particularly Björn and Benny as members of the Hootenanny Singers and The Hep Stars in the 1960s – had already devoted several summers to gruelling tours on the Swedish folkpark circuit, and felt that they had spent more than enough time on stage.

ABBA rehearsing before the first concert in Edmonton, September 1979.

Nevertheless, there was of course a huge demand for personal appearances by the group, and although promo films and the occasional TV show appearance seemed to be sufficent to sustain European interest in ABBA, the 1970s North American market worked a bit differently.

Before MTV was launched in the early 1980s, it was simply essential for artists to tour like crazy or frequently appear on TV shows; otherwise they were bound to make less impact in America than their competitors. Accordingly, history shows that despite ABBA's relative success in the North American market – especially Canada – they were never really able to conquer that territory in the same convincing way as they had conquered England or Australia.

ABBA's last tour had taken place in early 1977.

THERE HAD BEEN intermittent talk of a tour of North America from the time that ABBA first had a Top Ten hit in the United States with *Waterloo* in the summer of 1974; the intention at that time was to do a tour in early 1975. But a few years later, the group was still waiting for that final breakthrough before they went out on a tour, instead of doing it the other way around: touring in order to make a major impression on the American market.

Benny explained in an interview: "From the beginning, we said we did not want to go there as a supporting act for somebody else. We wanted to be the headliners." Björn added: "In all the other countries we've performed in we've already been big as a recording act. We'd all feel better if we could break the same way here. So far this system has worked in other countries, through television exposure and interviews."

In the spring of 1978 the first part of a two-step promotional campaign, geared towards raising awareness of ABBA in the United States, began. The most visible expressions were a huge billboard featuring the slogan "The largest selling group in the history of recorded music", which was erected above Sunset Strip in Los Angeles, and an appearance in an Olivia Newton-John TV special.

The result was that *ABBA – The Album* became ABBA's highest charting album ever on the US album charts, reaching #14, and that "Take A Chance On Me" became the group's second most successful single on the pop chart, peaking at #3 ("Dancing Queen" was ABBA's only US Number One).

The second step of the campaign was an extensive tour of North America in the autumn of 1979, which was followed by a trek around Europe. The tour had been planned in collaboration with tour promotor Thomas Johansson, and was originally meant to encompass Japan, the Far East, the Soviet Union and several Eastern European countries. However, the itinerary had to be shortened when sessions for the *Voulez-Vous* album dragged on.

Indeed, it was only when Björn and Benny went to the Bahamas for a couple of weeks in January 1979 that they were able to free their creativity and finally come up with the songs they were looking for. The songwriting couple stated that this was mainly because they finally got access to the popular music radio that was unavailable to them in Sweden.

"There was music available round the clock, whichever type you wanted to hear", explained Benny. "It goes without saying that it's incredibly inspiring when you get to hear a lot of fresh stuff that you like. You get a kick to try to do something yourself that is just as good as the things you hear."

As a result, after Björn and Benny had returned to Sweden, no less than half the songs on the album ("As Good As New", "Voulez-Vous", "I Have A Dream", "Does Your Mother Know" and "Kisses Of Fire") were recorded and finished within two months – it had taken eight months to produce the first batch of tracks. The Far East, the Soviet Union and Eastern Europe were removed completely from the tour itinerary, while the Japan dates were postponed until the spring of 1980.

When the *Voulez-Vous* album had been completed and released at the end of April 1979, ABBA put together a touring band consisting of their session musicians Lasse Wellander, guitar, Rutger Gunnarsson, bass and Ola Brunkert, drums, augmented by Mats Ronander, guitar, and Anders Eljas, keyboards. On 13th May – exactly four months before the first show of the tour in Canada – tentative rehearsals with the band started.

The reason for starting so early was that, having been away from the touring circuit for more than two years, the group felt a bit rusty as a live band. And they were now to tour a part of the world where ABBA were not major stars.

"We tour so infrequently that we need to have a little warm-up", explained Benny. "Especially since we're going to the United States, where we've never been before, and where we're all a bit unsure of how the audience regards us: whether they're familiar with us or not. We really don't know, so we need a little extra self-confidence as a stage act."

Agnetha looked forward to trying to conquer the US audience. "Canada has been very successful for us, but I guess America as a whole hasn't been that good", she reflected. "We are pretty spoilt with everything just going straight up. It's hard to achieve that kind of break in America. But it will be exciting to meet the audience, it's a real challenge."

For keyboardist Anders Eljas, who would come to play such a prominent part in Björn and Benny's post-ABBA careers, it was the second tour with the group. Through a series of lucky circumstances, he had come to play keyboards for singer Björn Skifs. Skifs, in the guise of Blue Swede, was the first Swedish artist to

Anders Eljas on tour with ABBA – the start of a working relationship with Björn and Benny that has continued to this day.

Agnetha on stage at the surprise concert in Landskrona, 18th May, 1979.

reach Number One on the US charts with *Hooked On A Feeling* in April 1974.

During the summer of 1976, Anders toured the folkparks with Skifs. Also on that tour was Claes af Geijerstam, who was to work as sound engineer on ABBA's tour in early 1977. He called Anders up and wondered if he would like to play keyboards on the ABBA tour. Anders of course said yes. "This was only my second job in this vein, so I missed out on all those running-out-of-gas experiences on some miserable tour in the north of Sweden, which every other musician has gone through. I started directly with the luxurious tours!"

For this 24-year-old, it was an overwhelming experience coming to the Europa Film studios for the first rehearsals. "I remember that there were a whole lot of impressions when I got there, because it was all so huge and kind of unreal." At the end of the day, however, it was just a matter of getting down to the job at hand: playing the music.

Singer Björn Skifs (right) gave ABBA the opportunity to try out their live band in front of an audience.

It was during the tour of Australia that Björn and Benny first noticed Anders' talents as an arranger. "When you're on tour there is something called 'the last gig goof', which is when you play a lot of practical jokes with the artists. The last song during the concert was a sort of unplugged version of "Thank You For The Music" when everybody was standing at the front of the stage. We had a string section during the Australian part of the tour, and they were only playing on a few numbers in the concert. I thought it was a pity that they weren't doing anything on the last song, so I wrote this string arrangement.

"When it came on, Benny was kind of startled and said, 'This is really great!' He thought that Rutger Gunnarsson had written it, because he did most of their arrangements, but Rutger told Benny that it was me. 'I didn't know you could read music', he said."

After the tour of Australia, Anders Eljas started getting work as arranger for many different recording sessions, and eventually his skills became fairly well-known in the music business. Anders' first official ABBA-related assignment came in the autumn of 1978 when he arranged strings and horns for the *Voulez-Vous* album tracks "The King Has Lost His Crown", "Angeleyes" and "If It Wasn't For The Nights". It became fairly self-evident that he would be an important part of the 1979 tour as well.

Björn, Benny and Agnetha in Landskrona.

This was also true of Anders Hanser, who, since those first studio pictures at the end of 1978, hadn't taken many pictures of ABBA. Yet when it was decided that the group was going on tour, he was invited to come along. Besides his being Görel's fiancé and a friend of the group, Polar and ABBA were again particularly keen to have him on board because his concert pictures of Rod Stewart had turned out so well.

ON 18TH AND 19TH MAY, 1979, surprise concerts were performed in Landskrona and Norrköping respectively, to try out the touring band in front of an audience. Anders Hanser was present at the concert with Björn Skifs at the discotheque Diskoland in Landskrona. The surprised audience witnessed how Björn suddenly left the stage and made way for ABBA instead. "It was the first time I saw ABBA live on stage, and it gave me a foretaste of what was to come during the autumn tour", remembers Anders.

During three weeks in August, the stage show was rehearsed at Europa Film Studios. By this time, the band had grown to include percussionist Åke Sundqvist as well as a trio of backing vocalists consisting of Tomas Ledin, Birgitta Wollgård and Liza Öhman. The backup singers had been asked along just a few weeks before the rehearsals started, and for Tomas Ledin, a star in his own right in Sweden, who had planned a trip abroad for the purpose of writing English-language songs, it was a chance to get a little inspiration for that task. In addition, the tour gave him the opportunity to perform one of his own songs, "Not Bad At All", which he'd written during rehearsals.

After two scrapped attempts earlier in the summer, ABBA tried to come up with a completely new song which they could release as a single in conjunction with the tour. They finally arrived at "Gimme! Gimme! Gimme! (A Man After Midnight)", which was recorded in August and released as a single in October. It ended up being one of ABBA's biggest chart hits of 1979.

The Landskrona audience got an unexpected chance to see ABBA live. Björn Skifs: "During the first two songs, the audience just stood there with their mouths wide open, they didn't know what was happening. Then they started cheering like crazy."

Scenes from the video for Gimme! Gimme! Gimme! (A Man After Midnight), Polar Music Studios, 5th September, 1979.

On 5th September, the same day the song was completed and mixed, a promo film directed by Lasse Hallström was made. Hallström had been the creator of all promo films for the group since their first, in 1974. He also directed the 1977 feature film *ABBA – The Movie*.

As usual when it came to visuals, the "Gimme! Gimme! Gimme!" video had to be done in a hurry. The chosen location was Polar Studios. Anders Hanser was also present and took some stills. Indeed, it was the "Gimme! Gimme! Gimme!" experience that made Anders realise that the best time for him to do his job as ABBA photographer was when the group were scheduled to appear in front of a camera anyway.

On the same occasion a promo film was made for "Estoy Soñando", the Spanish version of "I Have A Dream". It was ABBA's second Spanish recording of that year, the first being "Chiquitita", which had been particularly successful in the South American countries. Indeed, this first release had been put together at the request of RCA Records, who represented the group in South America. As the record company had predicted, the Spanish "Chiquitita" gave ABBA their definitive breakthrough in that territory.

When the roadies start pulling in all the equipment and putting it all together, that's when the show really begins. **Anders Eljas**

ON 13TH SEPTEMBER, 1979, ABBA's tour of North America commenced with a concert at Edmonton's Northlands Coliseum in Canada. The 15,000 tickets were sold out in one day when they were released in early August, and black market prices were around 200 dollars per ticket.

Arriving in Edmonton on the evening of 10th September, the group had a late night rehearsal on the 12th, and then ran through the show once more on the morning of the concert.

Anders Hanser photographed all of these events. "I had this idea from the beginning that I wanted to do a multi-image presentation of the pictures, so I decided to take as many pictures as possible, everywhere."

Although Stig Anderson always pointed out that Anders "must not forget to take black and white pictures!", Anders himself was more interested in taking colour photographs, especially during the actual concerts. "They were very colourful and beautifully lit, and the black and white pictures were only needed for newspapers and magazines."

Thomas Johansson – ABBA's invaluable tour promotor.

The ABBA backing band and backing vocalists, l-r: Lasse Wellander, Anders Eljas, Åke Sundqvist, Birgitta Wollgård, Tomas Ledin, Liza Öhman, Ola Brunkert, Rutger Gunnarsson and Mats Ronander.

ABBA are in town! ABBA and their crew prepare for the concert, while the audience is arriving and buying souvenirs.

Sound engineer Claes af Geijerstam, ABBA's good friend who beat them in the Swedish heats for the 1973 Eurovision Song Contest.

Åke Sundqvist, Lasse Wellander and Frida during rehearsals.

The main creator behind ABBA's 1979 stage design was Rune Söderqvist, inventor of the ABBA logo, and the group's album and single cover designer from the 1975 *Greatest Hits* album onwards. He remembers that the stage design presented him with a special sort of challenge.

Benny with set designer Rune Söderqvist.

"It was difficult to come up with a design that worked regardless of the size of the stage. We played for perhaps a few thousand people in one place and then 30,000 in another place. So I came up with a light-weight construction with canvas stretched over an aluminium frame, which was put on overlapping rails so that you could make it wide or narrow according to what was needed."

The idea behind the iceberg shapes in shades of blue, white and purple was that they should lead your thoughts to northern lights, as well as the name Polar Music and the Nordic countries in general; "the fact that we came from 'the top of the world'", as Rune puts it. Since the stage costumes had to be a part of the overall design, the 1979 tour marked the only time that Rune had the opportunity to work closely with costume designer Owe Sandström, who as usual came up with something colourful and certainly memorable for the members to wear.

Agnetha and Frida in their capes, meant to appear as a reflection of the polar mountains at the back of the stage.

I Have A Dream was performed with a different children's choir each night during the tour. On a couple of occasions, Agnetha was joined on stage by her daughter Linda.

Preparations backstage: Agnetha and Frida apply make-up and dress up in their stage costumes, while Benny and Rutger Gunnarsson enjoy a game of chess. Elisabeth Hofstedt was the hair stylist, while Ingmari Halling was responsible for the costumes.

Establishing himself as one of the major costume designers in Swedish show business in the early 1970s, Owe started working with ABBA very early on and is responsible for many of their best-known outfits. An example is Agnetha's and Frida's yellow and blue cat dresses, which were designed for the 1975 TV special *Made In Sweden*. The white jumpsuit with green and white cape as worn by Agnetha during the 1974/1975 tours and subsequent TV promo jobs, is another instantly recognisable item. This was the costume that helped Agnetha acquire the tag "the sexiest bottom in pop music".

Owe remembers very clearly how much preparation went into his and Rune Söderqvist's concept for the 1979 tour. "We used the last three colours of the rainbow – blue, indigo and violet – as the starting point for our designs. Then

we studied all ranges of colours imaginable; it's no exaggeration to say that we looked at several hundred different shades of those three colours. That led us on to the almost pink-purple shades that you see in the sky when the sun goes down, which gradually turn into violet and then dark blue. So those were the areas we were looking at to find our colours."

THE CAPES WORN BY Agnetha and Frida at the start of the show were the result of an idea Owe got from photographs he had taken in the high mountain areas in the north of Sweden.

"Those pictures were really beautiful and showed how the mountains reflected in the lake. I said, 'Why don't we use this idea? We have these gigantic mountain shapes in the background, and then the girls make their entrance with the polar mountains upside down on their capes, just like the reflections in a lake.'"

Another variation of the concept of diagonal lines to be found in the landscape of northern Sweden was the stripes flowing diagonally across Agnetha's and Frida's tricot costumes. In this case, the idea was that the stripes should represent a glacier. "The pattern on the costumes looks like a glacier-river flowing down, and it's almost exactly the same formations that you get in a glacier", says Owe Sandström.

Outside an arena during the US leg of ABBA's tour.

As the design concept for the show developed, some questions were raised as to whether the focus on icebergs and "cold" colours such as blue and violet would provide a chilly image. Both Owe and Rune felt that the fact that they used so many different shades in the design, combined with the lighting effects, meant that the end result was anything but cold.

THE FINAL STAGE CONSTRUCTION did not arrive for the première in Edmonton until the very last minute, since the first attempt to build it from the original design had been rejected. But any doubts Rune Söderqvist may have had as to whether the scenery would actually work visually were brushed aside when the tour party landed in Edmonton. "We were sitting in the bus from the airport when I suddenly saw some gigantic greenhouses that looked like glass pyramids, and they were all lit up. Then I thought: 'This is so right!'"

However, as he also remembers, the Nordic iceberg connection was somehow lost on certain North-American reviewers. "One review mentioned the stage design quite a lot because the writer thought that it was meant to evoke Indian tents. 'How very polite of them to think of that', he wrote."

In 1982, Rune's iceberg design also became the new Polar record label logo, a variation of which is used to this day on CD releases. "I didn't really like the northern lights type logo they used before, and I suggested that they should change it. You always sort of nag away at people and try to make things better. I'm still proud of that logo."

Stage designs aside, at the start of ABBA's first tour for two and a half years, the group members' level of apprehension varied somewhat. "This is going to be great. I'm not the least bit nervous", said Benny, while Björn, said to be the group member who worried the most about practical details, was less certain:

"Sure, everything has gone well and it's easy for people to say that there is nothing to worry about, but I do worry. In my head, I run through the songs and the show time and time again, and I wake up at nights worrying about starting to sing in the wrong place, or forgetting lyrics."

Frida, on the other hand, was perhaps the ABBA member who felt most comfortable on stage and got the greatest kick out of interacting with the audience. This was something she missed, and she was looking forward to the opportunity of leaving the recording studio and performing the ABBA songs live.

"When you're in the studio you work in a completely different way, because you're concentrating on creating the songs from scratch. But now that we've already recorded the songs, know how to sing them and are familiar with them – they've sort of become part of you – it'll be more fun to work with them live, because that's an altogether different feeling."

As it was, although the first half of the show was said by some to be a little stiff, the final impression of the Edmonton première concert was favourable.

ABBA on stage in front
of a full house.

The only immediate change in the set list after this first show was the removal of the poignant ballad "One Man, One Woman". According to a reviewer at the time, this performance of "what ought to have been a power-house of a song" simply didn't come off as it should in the show. A few concerts later, "Thank You For The Music" was also removed from the show, due to a muted response from audiences, while "Waterloo" was added as a final encore.

Immediately after the Edmonton concert, a triumphant ABBA held a press conference at the Four Seasons Hotel in front of 160 assembled media representatives from all over the world. For Anders Hanser, who was not really a press photographer, the press conferences during the tour were almost shocking experiences.

"I realised that photographers are very ruthless, and are all just out for themselves. But I thought, 'I can take my pictures later instead', so I often took pictures of the horde of photographers. It was slightly uncomfortable to have to stand in that crowd." Photographing the actual concerts was easier, but although all aspects of the shows were to be captured by Anders' camera, there was also a demand for solid pictures of the individual members in one contained shot. After the first few concerts, he'd realized that the only times during the concert that all four ABBA members were grouped together were during the songs "Hole In Your Soul" and "The Way Old Friends Do".

"I placed myself at the front, among the rest of the crowd, and that's a tough place to be standing while trying to take pictures. But to get the right feeling you really have to take the pictures from the front and stand right in the middle of the audience. I took whole sequences of pictures with a motor driven camera, and in that way you get every single movement."

IT WAS AT THE CONCERT at the Portland Opera House in Portland, Oregon on 18th September, that Anders' camera took the picture that famously ended up on a Swedish stamp four years later.

In 1983 the Swedish Post Office issued a set of stamps called *Musik i Sverige* ("Music In Sweden"), featuring famous representatives of the genres classical, jazz, folk, opera and pop. ABBA, of course, represented the last category.

The stamps were issued on World Music Day, 1st October, 1983 and were available until 31st December, 1983, marking the first time that a pop group

Frida performs "I Have A Dream"

was featured on such a prestigious forum. Apart from the royal family and a few sports stars such as Björn Borg, it was also the first time that living people were portrayed on a Swedish stamp.

Only Agnetha, Frida and Benny were taken from the original photograph, however, with the image of Björn playing guitar being inserted from another shot. "In the original picture none of the four has anything in their hands, but since the theme was 'music' the Post Office people wanted someone to be playing an instrument as well", explains Anders. The original photograph has become one of the most frequently used ABBA pictures, and as early as December 1979 it was featured on the cover of the single "I Have A Dream".

One of the ABBA members had to be playing something on the stamp issued by the Swedish Post Office in 1983, which is why two different pictures were used to make up the final image.

Touring with ABBA was apparently a very pleasurable experience, with little in the way of throwing TV sets out of hotel rooms and similar larks that rock stars mythically get up to. As Anders Eljas remembers, even the road crew was amazed at ABBA's unusual approach to touring.

"They were used to being treated like shit by most of the other big acts, but with ABBA it was different. The road crew should have their food, and we mustn't start the party before they had arrived, and so on, because those guys were working really hard. They thought that this was the best tour they had ever been on."

When the North American leg of the tour was concluded on 7th October the group had performed in Edmonton, Vancouver, Seattle, Portland, San Francisco, Los Angeles, San Diego, Phoenix, Las Vegas, Omaha, Minneapolis, Milwaukee, Chicago, New York, Boston, Montreal and Toronto.

However, the concert in Washington, DC, which was to have taken place between Boston and Montreal, had to be cancelled when Agnetha fell ill. A dose of the flu, in combination with an unusually shaky and scary flight with ABBA's plane, was too much for Agnetha.

"We flew one of those small private planes from New York to Boston and got caught up in absolutely terrible weather", she remembered later. "All the big planes had to turn back, but we didn't have enough fuel, so they had to find some place to let us land. When we were almost down on the airfield, all of a sudden they flew back up again. For one and a half hours our lives were in mortal danger – that's how it felt for me – with flashes on the wings, and nobody able to see anything. Everything was just black and the plane was shaking horribly. I prayed to God that I would not die."

I'm still alive, my life is rollin' on, gently from da
and my mind is slowly wakin', and my heart has ceased its a

The 1979 concerts featured Agnetha singing her own composition "I'm Still Alive",
featuring lyrics by Björn. The song has never been released on record.

**AND I DREAM I'M AN EAGLE,
AND I DREAM I CAN SPREAD
MY WINGS, FLYIN' HIGH, HIGH,
I'M A BIRD IN THE SKY**

The airport where ABBA's plane was supposed to land had been completely blown away by a tornado. After that traumatic experience, Agnetha performed the Boston concert through pure willpower, but she wasn't able to go through with the Washington concert.

When the time came to do the last two concerts in Montreal and Toronto, she'd sufficiently recovered to do them. "I wanted to show up at any cost for the audience there, although my legs were unsteady. They also showed up for me and that carried me through. When twelve thousand people in Montreal get up and wave and applaud, a wave of energy hits you. You are given strength and are rewarded for all the hard work, and it feels fantastic."

Björn performing "Does Your Mother Know".

"Why Did It Have To Be Me" was performed as a duet between Björn and Frida during the tour of North America and Europe. For this number, Frida dressed up in the sweater of one the local sports teams in each city ABBA visited.

After a one-and-a-half-week break in Stockholm, the European leg of the tour commenced. ABBA kicked off with a concert in Gothenburg on 19th October, continued through Stockholm, Denmark, France, The Netherlands, Germany, Switzerland, Austria, Belgium, England, Scotland, and finished the tour in Dublin, Ireland on 15th November.

The six concerts at Wembley Arena in London were to be an especially well documented part of the tour. A team from Swedish Television filmed the shows for an "in concert" TV special (a few scenes had also been shot in the United States). The sound was recorded and used for the TV special as well as a radio broadcast, and later also on the 1986 *ABBA Live* album. And of course Anders Hanser was there to take his pictures.

ANDERS' TOUR PHOTOGRAPHS were put to particularly good use a year later. In the summer of 1980, he wanted to create a multislide presentation based on his tour photographs and featuring a new ABBA song as the soundtrack. He was given "On And On And On", which was one of the finished tracks from ABBA's as yet unreleased *Super Trouper* album. Incidentally, the version Anders got featured a few extra lines that were edited from the recording before it was released on the album.

In late 1980, Anders' film for "On And On And On" – which was programmed by technician Peder Wistedt – even reached the general public when a few countries decided to release the track as a single. Since it wouldn't be a truly international release, Polar did not want to spend too much money on a video to accompany the single. Instead, they used Anders' slide presentation, which soon became the official video for the song.

In hindsight, ABBA's tour did not really achieve any major progress as far as their career in the United States was concerned. Rather, the tour seemed to confirm ABBA's status on the international music scene: in North America they had many dedicated fans but still found themselves just outside the circle of major stars, while in Europe it seemed they were able to fill enormous concert venues for several days in a row.

Certainly, Stig Anderson was well aware that this first US tour alone would not achieve a definite breakthrough in America for ABBA. "Of course, this is not a full scale attempt, because if you go for that, you have to cover the whole of this enormous country and stay here for three or four months", he explained.

"The situation here in the US is similar to the one we had in Australia once upon a time, in the sense that people are vaguely familiar with us: they have heard our records, they have seen us on TV, but it's not the same thing. In that respect, this tour has meant quite a lot for us, and I really wish we could go back at some point in the future and do it 'properly'."

The problem was that ABBA themselves were not especially interested in

touring or doing the follow-up appearances in the US that were demanded of them. After the two concluding tour weeks in Japan in March 1980, there were to be no more concerts as far as ABBA were concerned. The first few years of the new decade, which included the last three of the ABBA period, were to be characterised by significant steps away from all that had been typical of the group's 1970s career.

THE 1979 STAGE OUTFITS WERE among the last of Owe Sandström's many extraordinary ABBA creations over the past five years, and the clothes were henceforth primarily culled from the members' own wardrobes. The multi-layered sound and often somewhat impersonal lyrics that had been characteristic of ABBA's music were replaced by a more stripped-down soundscape and lyrics that more often reflected the group members' personal lives as they were at that time. Spectacular tours, feature films and extensive promotional appearances all around the world were replaced to an even greater extent by videos, interviews and TV specials, all produced in Sweden and then sent out over the world.

As is inevitable for most successful acts sooner or later, ABBA had reached the stage in their career when they felt it was time to slow down, enjoy the fruits of their labours and at the same time – perhaps on a subconscious level – start preparing themselves for the post-ABBA life they all knew must come sooner or later.

"Does Your Mother Know" gave Lasse Wellander an opportunity to shine with a guitar solo.

ABBA's musicians and backing vocalists, clockwise from top left: Mats Ronander and Tomas Ledin perform Ledin's "Not Bad At All"; Tomas Ledin, Birgitta Wollgård, Liza Öhman, Ola Brunkert, Åke Sundqvist, Rutger Gunnarsson, Lasse Wellander and Anders Eljas with Benny.

ABBA and their passionate fans.

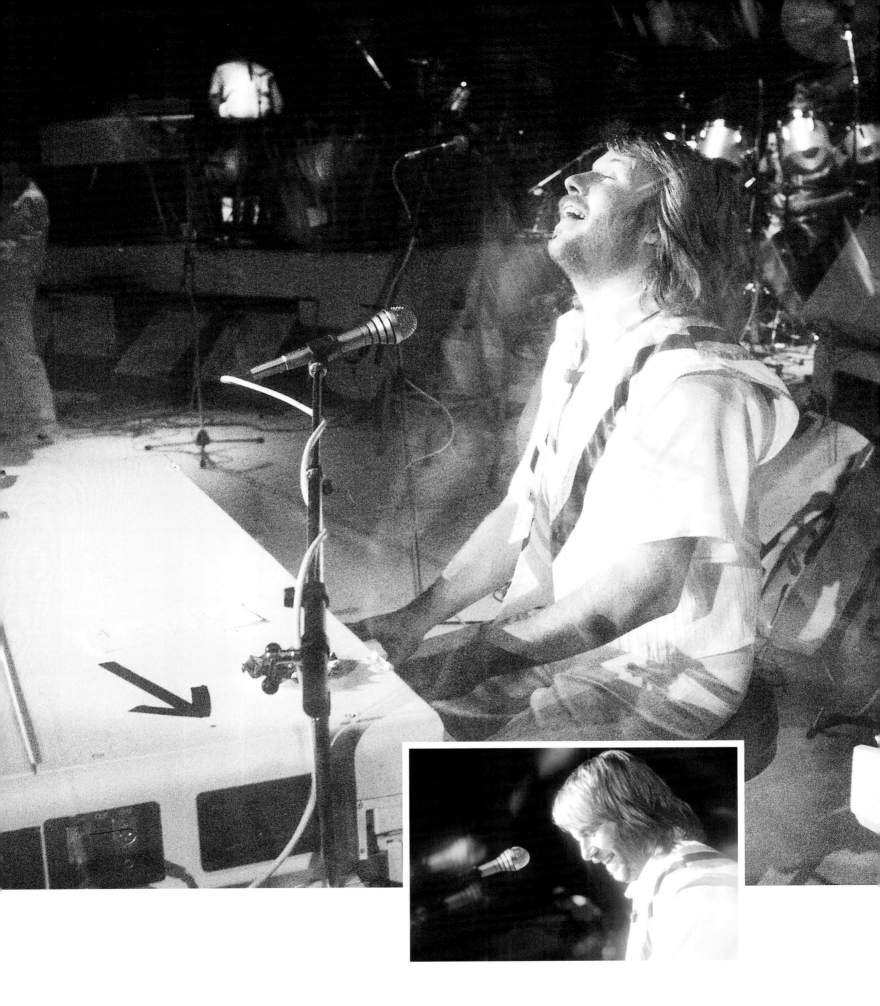

Agnetha relaxing in the tour bus.

Stig Anderson, ABBA and Thomas Johansson at the press conference after the Edmonton concert.

Stig Anderson
talks to a reporter.

During ABBA's six days
of shows at London's
Wembley Arena, Björn and
Benny appeared on the
UK TV show **Swap Shop**
and answered questions
in a live phone-in.

Björn and Stig at a party during the US part of the tour.

Stig with John Spalding, his longtime friend and business partner in the UK.

ABBA meet the Japanese press in Los Angeles.

Stig with Görel, always at the ready at his side.

Björn reads the reviews after the première concert in Edmonton.

Björn with TV presenter David Frost.

Björn, Frida, Benny and Britt Ekland at the after-show party in Los Angeles.

Stig Anderson and Görel Hanser, the president and vice-president of Polar.

Britt Ekland and Agnetha Fältskog in Los Angeles.

Björn greets the fans after one of the Wembley concerts.

Björn, Benny, Frida
and Agnetha with
daughter Linda,
relaxing by the pool
and water-skiing in
Vancouver, 16th
September, 1979.

Agnetha, Frida and Benny in the private plane ABBA used for flying between cities in the United States (top: with tour manager Bosse Norling; bottom: with Claes af Geijerstam).

wistfully reflect over what had been, rather than crying too many bitter tears over it. Interestingly, Agnetha has named this particular song as one of her major ABBA favourites – while Frida for her part has pointed out that she would have loved to have sung "The Winner Takes It All".

Both songs were typical of lyricist Björn's new tendency to write about subjects that meant something to him personally. "The Winner Takes It All" was somehow coloured by his divorce from Agnetha, while "Our Last Summer" was inspired by the memory of a girl in Paris he had a relationship with as a teenager. "It was a kind of melancholy memory of 'the last summer of innocence'", he said.

Anders Hanser's pictures from the Polar Studio in 1980 were taken while the group were recording the vocal over-dubs for "Our Last Summer". However, he never took any pictures while the tapes were actually rolling. "You had to be sensitive. I took my photographs while they were rehearsing, or listening to a playback. When they did an actual take, I kept a very low profile."

The vocal parts were usually perfected in one or two days – one day for harmony vocals and one day for the lead vocal – but these were very long days, where Agnetha and Frida worked until they dropped. The photographs from the "Our Last Summer" session give a very good picture of how work on a typical vocal overdub process would develop.

TO BEGIN WITH, ALL FOUR members gathered around the piano for Agnetha and Frida to get acquainted with the song. "They were remarkably talented when it came to absorbing the songs: that just went devastatingly quickly", says Michael Tretow.

When the two couples were still married, they had usually already heard the songs as they took shape at their respective homes. That way, some of the preparatory work could be done at home, before recording. Also at this time they would make sure that the song was in the right key for whoever was going to be the lead singer, suiting either Agnetha's soprano or Frida's mezzo-soprano voice.

The next step would be the lead vocalist putting down a preliminary vocal track, so that the melody was captured on tape when work on creating the harmony parts begun. "Arranging the harmony vocals was the major part of the work", says Michael. "'Should we accentuate the end of that word a little? In that case, both of us have to do it at the same time. Or should we try with you starting to sing there instead, and then you can back up that part', things like that. So the hard part was putting these finishing touches to the vocal arrangements."

The recording of the final lead vocal was left to last, to enable Frida and Agnetha to get even better acquainted with the song, thus helping them to put more feeling into the interpretation of the solo part. In the case of "Our Last Summer", Frida may possibly have recorded the finished lead vocal right at the start. The next day all pictures show Agnetha and Frida together at the microphones, or Agnetha alone. This suggests that they were primarily working on the backing vocals, and then went on to Agnetha's interpretation of "The Winner Takes It All".

Although as composers, arrangers and producers, Björn and Benny had a very clear vision of what they wanted the songs to be like, Agnetha and Frida were no puppets who just did as they were told. Benny has acknowledged many times that it was the combined sound of Agnetha's and Frida's voices that made up the largest part of the ABBA sound. Accordingly, arranging the vocals was very much a collaborative effort, where ideas popping up from any of the four members were considered. As always, the end result was all that mattered.

Agnetha and Frida recording the backing vocals for "Our Last Summer". Björn: "I remember that we worked a lot with the girls to get them to hold the notes on the word 'summer' in the chorus, in the way that American singers of the late 1950s would have done." Afterwards, the whole group and engineer Michael Tretow listen to the playback in the control room.

HOWEVER, ONE OCCASIONAL CAUSE of arguments would be Björn's and Benny's insistence that Agnetha and Frida should push their voices to the highest registers, almost beyond their ranges. Of course, both singers acknowledged that the results were stunning, and they were well aware of the special sound that was created by combining their two voices.

Michael Tretow has pointed out many times that not only did Frida and Agnetha have the talent to wrap their voices around the most difficult vocal parts, but they were also able not to let their ability for precision stand in the way of their interpretation.

"This often happens with professional backing singers, who normally are able to sing anything from a technical point of view, but with Frida and Agnetha you had the added ability to make every part of their vocal performance sound like they really meant what they were singing."

Although from the outside it may look as if the glitter and glamour, or having an audience of tens of thousands in the palm of your hand during a live concert, would be what gave a performer the greatest kick, Agnetha and Frida both shared Björn's and Benny's preference for working in the recording studio. As Agnetha has pointed out, "To participate in the creation of the songs and try to interpret them in your own way was the best part of being in ABBA."

I don't wanna talk about the things we've gone through

THE WINNER TAKES IT ALL *making of promo film, Marstrand, 12th July, 1980*

WITH SEVEN SONGS FOR THE forthcoming *Super Trouper* album in the can, ABBA felt it was time to release a single as a foretaste. The choice was "The Winner Takes It All", and director Lasse Hallström was commissioned to make a video, or promo film as those short clips were still called at the time.

Hallström had been the director of ABBA's promo films since the very first, "Waterloo" and "Ring Ring", which were both made in the summer of 1974. This was way before million-dollar budget videos became the industry standard in the 1980s. Both songs were actually filmed on the same day.

The son of a dentist who enjoyed making 8mm amateur films in his spare time, Lasse Hallström was a pupil at the Adolf Fredrik music high school in the early 1960s. There, Lasse started making his own 8mm movies together with some fellow students. "The films were parodies of prominent directors of the day, like Antonioni, Bergman and Fellini, and we showed them in the school assembly hall", he remembers.

Anders Hanser, one year older than Lasse, was a pupil at the very same school around the same time. "I was the photographer at school and Lasse was the filmmaker", he says. "Quite a lot of pupils at the school had creative inclinations, and many of them have since gone on to careers in the world of media and showbusiness."

A few of Lasse's friends from school formed a pop group called The Mascots, who became one of the most popular bands in Sweden in the mid-1960s. Lasse made a half-hour long film in which the group performed some of their songs. "I rented a 16mm camera and it became my first professional film. It turned out that Swedish Radio wanted to buy the film and show it, and in that way I got a foot in the door in their television department."

ABBA at the Society House in Marstrand during the making of the video for "The Winner Takes It All".

Agnetha on location in Marstrand. In the video for "The Winner Takes It All" she acted the part of a woman coming to terms with the end of a relationship.

In 1967, Lasse Hallström started doing freelance work for television, directing short film clips of pop acts performing songs, which were to be shown on a music show called *Popside*. "It could be anyone from current Swedish groups to foreign guests like The Move or The Hollies", he recalls.

This was where he perfected his skills of making simple but effective promo clips on a very low budget – and very quickly. "When those foreign groups got here I had perhaps two hours to film one song, so you didn't really have time to film them in too many different environments. We would just sort of traipse out on the big field outside the TV studios and try to put something together."

AROUND THIS TIME, he also did some work trying to salvage a somewhat unstructured film project, provisionally titled *Habari Safari*, which Benny's group The Hep Stars had begun working on in Africa in early 1967. "That's when I met Benny for the first time. They'd gone to Africa and come back home with something fragmentary, that I tried to piece together. I remember filming them performing some songs, but in the end the results were never shown."

By the early 1970s, Hallström was employed by Swedish Radio, and started filming short comedy skits that originally were to be shown in between the pop clips. He collaborated with comedians Magnus Härenstam and Brasse Brännström on these productions. They soon became very popular in their own right. Björn Ulvaeus remembers that it was through these skits that ABBA became interested in hiring Lasse as director of their promo clips.

Lasse Hallström ended up directing all of ABBA's official videos except "Chiquitita", Anders Hanser's photo collage for "On And On And On", and the two very last videos in 1982. The budget was always fairly modest, and consequently, the ideas for presenting the group in the film had to be quite basic as well. This was when Lasse's experience, working wonders with limited resources, came in very handy.

"Apart from writing the storyboard and directing, I was also the photographer all through these years, except for the very last clips", he recalls. "There were only three people involved: myself, a guy who ran the playback tape, and someone who took care of the lighting."

On several occasions over the years, Lasse managed to complete two promo films in one day. He'd get a tape of the songs a few days beforehand and start to sketch out some ideas for a storyboard. "We had such a short amount of time, so I had to be prepared and come up with some ideas beforehand. There wasn't time to film them in any more than three different locations."

For ABBA themselves, the most important plus of making the films was cutting down on their personal television appearances – and just like when Anders Hanser was taking his pictures, Björn and Benny liked things to be over and done with fairly quickly. "They didn't have very much patience for

Anders Hanser tried out a new soft filter when he took some portraits of ABBA. Lasse Hallström borrowed the filter and used it in a few scenes in the video.

this", recalls Lasse. "Benny used to joke that he only had two different facial expressions anyway."

The group members seldom interfered with the look of the films much. "As I remember it, they weren't really involved in the ideas or storyboards for the films. They had neither the time nor the inclination to do that. We would perhaps talk on the phone, discussing the clothes, although I was never involved in actually deciding what they should be wearing. Then they would just show up wherever we were going to shoot."

Many of the tricks and effects Lasse was to use most frequently with ABBA could be spotted during the earliest productions. For instance, the 1975 *Mamma Mia* film introduced the legendary close-up shots with two group members, one of whom was shown full face and the other in profile, and also the grouping of members in different combinations of pairs, contrasting one against the other.

Although quite a few prominent acts before ABBA – such as The Beatles – had taken to making special promo clips for their current singles, they'd generally

only started doing so after they'd already become internationally successful. It's probably true, then, that ABBA were among the first artists to benefit from sending out these films to TV stations over the world at a very early stage in their career, as opposed to building up interest primarily through the routine of touring and personal apperances.

"BJÖRN AND BENNY TELL ME that they'd never have been as successful in Australia if it hadn't been for those videos", Lasse Hallström points out. It was indeed when the promotional films for "I Do, I Do, I Do, I Do, I Do" and "Mamma Mia" were shown on the Australian television show *Countdown* in 1975 that the country was struck by ABBA fever. At that time, the group had never even set foot in Australia.

In that respect, ABBA truly were video pioneers, for it was not until the 1980s and the MTV explosion that the method of systematically building up pop careers with the help of big budget videos became an integral part of the music business machinery.

BY THE TIME THE FILM for "The Winner Takes It All" was made, the budget for ABBA videos had increased enough to allow for them to spend one whole day on a single film. In the summer of 1980, Lasse Hallström was working in the town of Marstrand on the west coast of Sweden, making the movie *Tuppen* ("The Rooster"), which meant that ABBA had to travel there on 12th July in

Video director Lasse Hallström pouring champagne for ABBA.

order to film their promo clip. "Benny and Frida happened to be in the nearby Gothenburg archipelago anyway, so it was convenient", says Hallström.

Anders Hanser, who photographed the occasion, was not actually commissioned to do so by Polar. "Görel and I happened to be on holiday on the west coast, and decided to go down there. I thought, 'I might as well take a few pictures while I'm there'." By chance, he also had a new soft filter with him that he wanted to try out. Lasse Hallström borrowed it, and that's why both Anders' pictures and some of the shots in the promo film have a similar softened effect.

ABBA on the balcony of the Society House.

The film for "The Winner Takes It All" was shot on various outdoor locations in Marstrand, with interior scenes being filmed in the Society House. The clip featured Agnetha acting the part of a woman coming to terms with the end of a love affair and reminiscing about happier times, tying in with the song's lyrics. To underline this theme, the film started and ended with a collage of black and white pictures of ABBA. "I wanted to create some kind of nostalgic shimmer of memories of times long past", recalls Lasse Hallström.

Although compared with today's million-dollar video extravaganzas, Lasse Hallström's ABBA videos may seem fairly basic and simple, he is still proud of most of them, naming "Money, Money, Money" as one of his favourites.

"That one turned out really well; it was consistent with the lyrics and the music. I loved editing my films to fit the music, to emphasize the rhythm and the idea of the music, to provide musical support and not just tell a story. When I watch MTV today I feel like this really conservative old pop-film-maker, because I think there's too little support for the music and the rhythm. I get the feeling that many of the films tell their stories on a separate, parallel track, they don't really accompany the song."

Anders Hanser makes a similar observation: "You can't help being amazed by the simple yet skilful tricks Lasse was employing. That's the strength of those ABBA films. Today's video producers wouldn't believe their ears if you told them what the budget limitations were. But within those means he managed to create videos that were never repetitive and that still stand up well."

Already a prominent director in Sweden by the late 1970s, Lasse Hallström would go on to achieve international fame with his 1985 movie *My Life As A Dog*. During the 1990s, he has directed pictures such as *What's Eating Gilbert Grape*, *Grace Under Pressure* and the Oscar-winner *The Cider House Rules*.

WHEN BJÖRN, BENNY, MICHAEL TRETOW and the session musicians entered the studio to record "The Winner Takes It All" on 2nd June, 1980, the song had the working title "The Story Of My Life". Most of ABBA's songs originally had a completely different title, since Björn usually started by putting together demo lyrics that could be sung while the instrumental backing track was arranged and recorded. Only when the backing track was finished did Björn consider himself able to "feel" what the song was really about, and write the proper lyrics.

The first attempt to record a backing track for "The Story Of My Life" turned out much too stiff and square, however. Both Björn and Benny felt that this was a song with great potential, and therefore it was especially important that the opportunity to record it in the right way was not wasted. The problem was solved when Benny came up with the piano melody lines that tie the different parts of the song together, thereby opening it up for the looser, chanson-like arrangement that was recorded a few days later.

ABBA was not normally a group that used drink or drugs to stimulate creativity, but Björn has revealed that the lyrics for "The Winner Takes It All" – where the divorce theme meant something to him personally – were written with the aid of a bottle of whisky.

"I was drunk and the whole lyric came to me in a rush of emotion in one hour. And that never works. You think it's wonderful at the time but it looks terrible the next day, but that one worked." As Björn remembers it, tears were flowing in the recording studio after Agnetha had recorded her lead vocal.

"The Winner Takes It All" is without doubt one of ABBA's very best songs, and it has remained a favourite for all four members of the group. The single was released on 21st July, 1980 and became a huge success all over the world.

Photographer Lars Larsson at the top of the ladder, directing the **Super Trouper** cover photo session.

Smiling, having fun, feeling like a number one

SUPER TROUPER *cover photo session and making of promo film, Europa Film Studio, October 1980*

BY AUGUST 1980, BJÖRN AND BENNY were hard at work again, writing further songs for the new album. During September, the group recorded the tracks "Me And I" and "Lay All Your Love On Me". Since the live recording of the song "The Way Old Friends Do", made at London's Wembley Arena in November 1979, had also been slated for inclusion, the album was now considered a completed project. It was also high time to finish off the recording sessions if the album was to reach record dealers in time for Christmas.

By mid-September, it had been decided that the LP was to be called *Super Trouper*, referring to the gigantic spotlights used for stadium concerts. Album designer Rune Söderqvist and photographer Lars Larsson associated these spotlights with circuses, however, and that's how they came up with the motif that was featured on the cover.

ABBA were surrounded by friends during the **Super Trouper** photo session. Immediately in front of them, dressed in white, is Polar label manager Hans Bergkvist; to the left with a headband is Lillebil Ankarcrona (sister of Benny's current wife Mona), looking at Görel Hanser; singer Tomas Ledin is standing fairly close to the right of Benny wearing a hat with a feather in it.

Rune Söderqvist had been ABBA's album and single cover designer since late 1975. Trained as an art director during the 1950s, he worked as creative director at various advertising companies through the 1960s. When he realised that he was starting to become an administrator rather than the creative artist he wanted to be, he left the advertising business and started his own design studio.

Rune entered the ABBA circle through an acquaintance with photographer Ola Lager, who had taken the cover pictures for the 1974 *Waterloo* album as well as the 1975 *ABBA* album. "I often worked with Ola at that time, and I suggested to him that ABBA might need a logo. Ron Spaulding, the art director they'd mostly been working with previously, had moved to Thailand, and when Ola told them what I'd said, I got the job."

Album cover designer Rune Söderqvist in discussion with circus director François Bronett and photographer Lars Larsson, as well as with Björn and Benny.

Rune Söderqvist started his association with ABBA by designing the sleeve for their 1975 *Greatest Hits* album, but the first cover to be adorned by the new ABBA logo with the backwards B was the *Dancing Queen* single, released in August 1976. Rune recalls that it wasn't easy to come up with the right design for this trademark.

"That's one of the hardest tasks you can get, because a logo has to be very minimalistic and yet it must signify so many things. But after agonising over it a bit I suddenly realised that 'this is how it must be, this is logical – these two couples belong together, and so each B should be turned towards each A'. Then it was just a matter of coming up with the right typeface."

THE RIGHT TYPEFACE turned out to be the fairly strict and sober News Gothic Bold. Indeed, unusually for something designed in the post-flower power 1970s, the ABBA logo was anything but extravagant, colourful or embellished. "That was probably because I was schooled in the pop and op art of the 1960s", says Rune. "I still feel that was the best decade in the modern age in terms of graphic art, but also in other design areas. I guess that was why I didn't go for all that embellishment."

Rune remembers that Benny was the only ABBA member to take any great interest in the look of the logo, and he was a bit unsure if the restrained, unadorned approach was the right way to go. "He said, 'Isn't it a bit too industrial-looking?' But in the end he accepted my argument that I knew what was needed since I was the one who was going to be using it."

Apart from creating the logo, as far as Rune was concerned the "Dancing Queen" single cover was simply a matter of taking an already existing picture and conjuring up a design. The first time he was involved with the concept from the beginning was when he designed the sleeve for the *Arrival* album, released in the autumn of 1976.

Stig Anderson's youngest son Anders, Görel Hanser with friend Fernando, singer Björn Skifs with producer Bengt Palmers and Tomas Ledin were all present when the cover for the **Super Trouper** album was shot.

ABBA during a break of the making of the "Super Trouper" video.

It was always hard to come up with a good way to present four people on an album cover, but Rune got the idea that it would look great to put the four members together in a helicopter. Also, his then wife Lillebil (sister of Benny's current wife Mona) thought that *Arrival* would be a good name for an album, and that was also how an untitled, instrumental track that ABBA had been working on at the end of the album sessions got its title.

Over the following years, Rune Söderqvist continued designing single and album covers for ABBA and other Polar artists. When the time came to do the *Super Trouper* album cover, the ever-busy ABBA left it to Rune to come up with a suitable concept.

"As usual, they were working in the studio and didn't have the time to deal with stuff like that, but all the same a cover had to be made. We knew that we would have quite a high budget for the album cover since a promo film was to be made at the same time, and then we had the idea that we should do the photo shoot at Piccadilly Circus in London."

The location being chosen for no other reason than the fact that there was a "circus" connection in the name, the intention was to feature ABBA surrounded by a big crowd of circus performers and animals in the cover picture. Rune and tour promotor Thomas Johansson went over to London to make arrangements.

"We met a number of people who would arrange the circus for us, and we also met the Chief Constable of London. He was a bit cautious as he feared it would be chaotic with all these people there. We said, 'We'll just shoot it at three o' clock in the morning when nobody is there'. My plan was that we would leak the information anyway, because I wanted to have as many people as possible there."

As it turned out, there was a law against entertainers or animals appearing in central London. Apparently, this was to prevent the many theatres in the area setting up publicity stunts.

The end result: Lars Larsson's picture on the cover of the **Super Trouper** album.

Some time later, the scenes featuring ABBA actually singing "Super Trouper" were shot at Europa Film Studios.

Stills of the individual members were used to create a stop-motion effect in the "Super Trouper" video.

"The Chief Constable said that we could of course take our chances and do it anyway. But when we got home, Polar didn't dare to go through with it because it would cost too much if the police stopped it – which was almost what I was hoping for. The group was very determined not to be mixed up in any scandals, so London was out."

Instead, the Europa Film Studio was booked for the evening of 3rd October, and ABBA and their friends brought together as many acquaintances as they could find, all of whom dressed up in "festive" costumes. Rune also hired two circuses – with almost disastrous results. "When everybody was made up and ready it turned out that one of the circuses had left, because they were enemies with the other circus. So I had to make do with what I had."

Originally, there were to have been many more circus artists featured in the picture, to give the sense of a really big crowd, but it was felt that they'd have drawn too much attention away from the group. "As you can see in the finished cover picture, all the lights are on the group, and everything else was moved further and further away from them: all the fire-eaters, acrobats and whatever.

But it worked, even though it didn't turn out exactly the way we'd planned it from the beginning. It almost never does."

Rune Söderqvist points out that it was always important to come up with a simple but effective concept where ABBA could just pose as themselves in the picture. "In this case it works really well, because it feels like this is 'after the performance' or that they are attending their own première, or something like that." Indeed, the festive atmosphere of the filmed scenes made them suitable for inclusion in the video for the song "Happy New Year" as well.

While Rune and his team were planning the cover shoot, Björn and Benny had started feeling that they should perhaps try to come up with one more song for the album, something really strong that would work as a single that could be released in conjunction with the LP. The musicians were booked for 3rd October – the same date that had been set for the evening circus photo session – and for a couple of days before the recording sessions, Björn and Benny sat down in the studio and wrote a new song. The result was "Super Trouper".

"We hadn't planned to call the new song 'Super Trouper' as well, but strangely enough, those words just happened to fit", Björn later recalled. Even if the title was there, the finished

lyrics didn't come at once – it was a deceptively difficult task to come up with lyrics about a spotlight – and when the group were being filmed and photographed at Europa Film, the song still had the working title *Blinka lilla stjärna* ("Twinkle, Twinkle, Little Star").

Consequently, the scenes in the "Super Trouper" promo film, where ABBA are seen miming to the song, were filmed at a later date when the final lyrics had been written and recorded. Incidentally, these scenes also contained still photography sequences that were put together from pictures that Anders Hanser took during the filming.

The *Super Trouper* album was released 3rd November, 1980, occupying the Number One spot for four weeks on the Swedish charts, while the single of the same name was released a couple of weeks later.

No more champagne, and the fireworks are through

HAPPY NEW YEAR *making of promo film, 8th November, 1980*

ONE OF THE FIRST SONGS to be written and recorded for the *Super Trouper* album was "Happy New Year". Björn and Benny had dreamt for several years of writing a musical, and before the start of virtually every album project over the past few years they'd told themselves, "Now we are going to do it".

This was also true of the songwriting period that resulted in the *Super Trouper* album, and when the composing team went on a songwriting trip to Barbados in January 1980, they got the idea for a musical that was to take place on New Year's Eve. "We thought it would be a good framework: a few people in a room, looking back on what has been, thinking about the future, that sort of thing", Benny recalled.

In Barbados they happened to run into the comedian John Cleese, and had dinner with him. However, their suggestion that he should write the book for the musical did not interest Cleese very much. The only result of these ideas for a New Year's Eve musical was the song "Happy New Year", recorded during the first batch of sessions for the *Super Trouper* album.

On 8th November, 1980, a video was made for the song in Lasse Hallström's apartment in Stockholm. "That was simply for practical reasons", says Lasse. "I had a very big apartment, much bigger than I needed, so I thought I might as well make use of it. I wanted to keep things as simple as possible."

On this particular occasion, Hallström's inclination to work from home led to some fairly comical consequences. "Tommy Körberg was staying at my place at the time. He had been out late the night before, and woke up and heard this

The videos for "Happy New Year" and its Spanish version "Felicidad" were made in Lasse Hallström's apartment.

Lasse Hallström, at the camera, tried out yet another of his many camera tricks: "We put the girls and the guys in one of these huge flower pots with wheels on it, and then a friend of mine sat on the floor and turned it around and around. It was a pretty absurd sight."

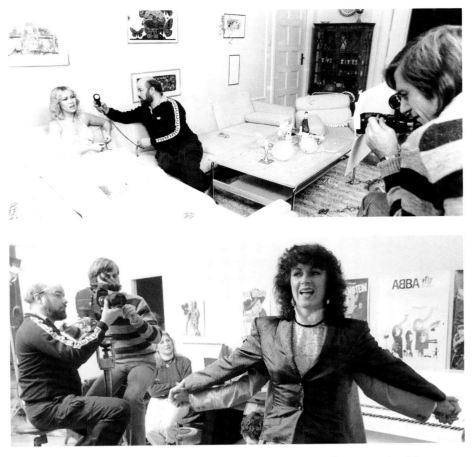

"happy new year, happy new year" being sung over and over again. He got up to find out what was going on, and ended up crashing right into the scenery."

"Happy New Year" was never an international single release for ABBA, and it seems a tad curious that this video was ever made. However, during the spring of 1980 there had been talk of the song being released as a single in conjunction with the release of the forthcoming album, and it's possible that at this stage, "Happy New Year" was considered as a potential follow-up to the "Super Trouper" single.

WHILE THEY WERE AT IT, a video was also made for "Felicidad", the Spanish version of "Happy New Year". The previous year's success with the Spanish recordings of "Chiquitita" and "I Have A Dream" had led to the recording of a whole album of Spanish versions of well-known ABBA songs. The album was titled *Gracias Por La Música* and turned out to be fairly successful as well.

When the *Super Trouper* album was recorded, it was decided that two Spanish-language tracks were to be included on the South American release. The chosen tracks were "Happy New Year" and "Andante, Andante".

Although "Happy New Year" never became a hit single, its New Year's Eve theme has made it a very popular end-of-year song – and perhaps the closest ABBA ever came to a Christmas song.

ABBA and Stig Anderson at the Polar offices.

Hova's witness – full speed ahead
ABBA and Stig Anderson

HOVAS VITTNE *making of video at Berns, 24th January, 1981*

STIG ANDERSON'S 50TH BIRTHDAY *Villa Ekarne, 25th January, 1981*

MIDSUMMER AT VIGGSÖ *Early 1980s*

GOLDEN GRAMOPHONE AWARD, *11th October, 1982*

WHEN GÖREL HANSER celebrated her 30th birthday in June 1979, ABBA and Stig Anderson recorded a special tribute called "Sång till Görel" ("Song For Görel"). This recording was pressed up on a strictly limited edition 12-inch single and given to guests at Görel's party. Some one and a half years later, Stig Anderson turned 50 and ABBA naturally wanted to put together a special musical celebration for him as well.

Björn and Benny wrote a song entitled "Hovas vittne" ("Hova's Witness"), a play on words referring to Hova, the place where Stig was born and raised. The humorous lyrics, written by the four ABBA members, sound engineer Michael Tretow and album cover designer Rune Söderqvist, contained references to Stig's dog Lucas, his love for all kinds of sausages, and his penchant for raising the key a semi-tone at a certain point in a song, something ABBA actually do while singing about it in the song's bridge.

Rune Söderqvist remembers that the lyrics were arrived at by sitting down, ad-libbing ideas and coming up with stories that captured Stig's personality. One quaint characteristic detailed in the lyrics concerned Stig's habit of star-

Stig Anderson at the Polar offices, June 1982.

ABBA, dressed up in their Waterloo costumes, tape the video for the tribute song "Hovas vittne" at the Berns restaurant, 24th January, 1981. "Sticket" refers to the "bridge" section of a song, which ABBA are singing about in the lyrics.

ting the vacuum cleaner when he wanted his guests to leave his parties.

"When he got tired of his guests – no matter who it was – he would bring out the vacuum cleaner and announce loudly: 'The taxi cabs are here!' Because he'd called for cabs as well", confirms Rune Söderqvist. "Of course, it was a bit embarrassing to stay then."

THE SONG WAS RECORDED about a week before Stig's birthday at Polar Music studios, and was pressed in 200 red vinyl copies only. An instrumental version of his first hit, "Tivedshambo", was featured on the B-side. The day before Stig's birthday, a special video for the song, directed by Kurt Hjelte, was taped at the Stockholm show venue Berns, featuring ABBA dressed up in their 1974 "Waterloo" costumes.

On his 50th birthday, Stig Anderson and his wife Gudrun were woken up by the singing of a ladies choir, augmented by Björn and Benny. The members of the choir were Agnetha, Frida, Lena Ulvaeus, Görel Hanser, Lillebil Ankarcrona, Anita Axelsson and Marianne Andersson. Rune Söderqvist: "Stig loved net stockings, so it was perfect that they came in there and danced a little."

Later during the party, the male choir Mansläpparna performed together with the female choir. Björn, Benny, Rune Söderqvist, Lasse Hallström and Tomas Ledin were among the members of Mansläpparna.

During parties, there was usually a jazzy jam session. In these pictures, Benny, Stig Anderson, John Spalding and Björn Ulvaeus provide entertainment at the wedding party for Stig's daughter Marie and Tomas Ledin.

FOR BIRTHDAY BOY Stig Erik Leopold Anderson, celebrations on 25th January started with a big surprise. At seven o'clock in the morning, a ladies choir consisting of among others Frida, Agnetha, Björn's wife Lena and Görel Hanser strode into Stig's bedroom. The choir was singing specially-written birthday lyrics to the melody of the 1969 hit "Ljuva sextital" ("The Good Old Sixties"), originally written by Björn, Benny and Stig.

He'd hardly recovered from that shock when Björn and Benny climbed in through the window singing a traditional Swedish birthday song, accompanied by Benny's accordion.

Later, during the party that followed, the recording and video performance of "Hovas vittne" was presented. The publishing contract for the song was also given to Stig, attached with one single condition: that it should never be recorded with any other lyrics than the heartily sarcastic lines put together by the ABBA members and their friends.

Music publishing being an integral part of Stig's life, he later couldn't keep himself from remarking that it was a pity that such a good song could not be used for any other purposes.

In some respects, Stig's 50th birthday celebrations proved to be the peak of the friendship and close working relationship between Stig and the ABBA members. Soon afterwards, Stig moved away from the music side of his company, instead immersing himself in investing the vast earnings from ABBA's records in various business ventures. ABBA themselves were naturally more concerned with the music, and felt a bit uncomfortable being tagged as "investors" by the media because of their connection to Polar.

As Görel Hanser watches, Björn and Benny hand over the publishing contract for Hovas vittne to Stig Anderson at his 50th birthday party.

The flag is lowered on Viggsö.

Stig Anderson enjoyed playing his guitar on festive occasions.

ONE IMPORTANT ASPECT OF THE close relationship between Stig and ABBA had been the summers spent at the island of Viggsö in the Stockholm archipelago, where they all had houses. This was their base during the summers, and a place where they could find time both to relax and to get some work done.

Stig had been the first in the gang to get a house on Viggsö, and he'd often sit there churning out Swedish lyrics for songs he'd purchased from abroad so that they could be recorded by Swedish artists. For their part, Björn and Benny would sit in their songwriting cottage – which actually belonged to Björn – and write hit songs for ABBA.

At Viggsö, the extended Polar and ABBA "family" would also celebrate the traditional Swedish Midsummer at the end of June. On the eve of Midsummer Day – the day with the most daylight hours of the year – most Swedes get together for a day of festivities, eating traditional food such as herring, dancing around the maypole, and generally just having a good time with friends and family.

Björn with his son Christian at Viggsö.

Midsummer dancing around the maypole with Björn, Stig Anderson, Lasse Wellander and Benny.

PART OF A SUCCESS THAT NEVER ENDS

IN OCTOBER 1982, ABBA WERE awarded the Golden Gramophone by Polydor at a ceremony at the Polar offices in Stockholm. The Golden Gramophone was given to "famous artists who over the years have been faithful to Polydor International […], who have made numerous recordings of an artistically excellent quality and who are known around the world for their service to music." ABBA had been chosen as the recipients this year particularly for "their success as top selling act on the Polydor label in 1981".

It was also during this occasion that Björn, Benny and Stig got to hear the sound of a compact disc for the first time. *The Visitors*, being ABBA's most recent album – and also digitally recorded for the most part – had been issued as one of the very first CDs, and the Polydor people had brought a copy with them.

However, three tracks on the album had been recorded on analogue equipment – Polar Studios got their first digital recorders a few months into sessions for the album – and therefore there was an audible hiss in the segue between the analogue recording "Slipping Through My Fingers" and the digital track "Like An Angel" Passing Through My Room".

Björn, Benny and Stig are awarded the Golden Gramophone at the Polar offices. Together with PolyGram boss Jan Timmer, they also take a listen to the very first ABBA CD, **The Visitors**.

Why don't we meet for a chat

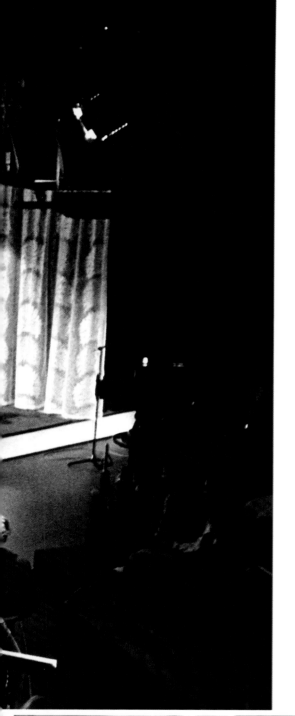

IN MID-MARCH 1981, ABBA started recording what was to be their last album, *The Visitors*. The first recording period was concluded a month later, after which the group started preparing a TV special.

Dick Cavett Meets ABBA was originally to have been a look back on the group's career, where old video clips were interspersed with new material. That idea was abandoned, however, and instead the special was divided into two segments. In the first part, Dick Cavett, one of the biggest talk show names in the United States at the time, made small talk with the four ABBA members. There then followed a live concert – featuring the same backing band that ABBA had used on their 1979 concert tour – where nine songs were performed.

When the special was broadcast, only a selection of these songs were shown in most countries, though all of them were included in at least one of these versions. Among the songs that were performed, "Gimme! Gimme! Gimme! (A Man After Midnight)", "Super Trouper", "Two For The Price Of One" and "On And On And On" were also released on the 1986 album *ABBA Live*, while "Slipping Through My Fingers" and "Me And I" appeared on the 1994 *Thank You For The Music* CD box set. Only the versions of "Knowing Me, Knowing You", "Summer Night City" and "Thank You For The Music" remain unreleased on record to this day.

Dick Cavett Meets ABBA was a co-production between Polar and Swedish Television, and was a typical example of ABBA's later tendency to base their promotional activities in Sweden as much as possible, and then send the finished product out over the world.

Anders Hanser was present in the studio, documenting the work on the TV special from start to finish. There were tentative plans to publish a book based on his pictures, but this ultimately never happened.

ABBA preparing backstage and then meeting the press together with Dick Cavett.

Rehearsals for the concert part of the **Dick Cavett Meets ABBA** TV special.

DC: There has probably never been a musical act in the history of the business who has had quite the success in certain ways as this group has. Why is ABBA so popular?

BJÖRN: Actually, we don't know. We're just doing the things we're doing. Writing the songs and recording them as well as we can. And this is what happens. It's crazy, but it's true.

FRIDA: It must be something that has to do with the music, the melodies.

BENNY: It's a very difficult question to answer. It's many small things put together. We're well organized and get good support from all the record companies. It's a lot of hard work.

AGNETHA: We've thought about this many times, but we've never come to a conclusion. It may be because we always sing our own songs and that we are perfectionists, all of us.

BJÖRN: We've always liked a strong melody. I guess that's a European tradition more than an ~~inri~~ American one. That seems to go down well.

DC: To put it politely, people seldom rave about your lyrics, but they do about the melodies. Aren't you sensitive to the criticism that the lyrics are unmemorable?

BJÖRN: I would not say that ~~it's~~ (that's) true nowadays. It was true to some extent before. We used to use the words as something you had to have to sing the melody and they did not mean very much to us. But I would say that the lyrics on the last two albums have improved. We try to put more feeling into them ~~words~~.

DC: People think of you primarily as musical. There must be times when you want to get away from it all, from composing, ~~frxx~~ recording, performing, thinking about music. What do you do that's utterly unmusical to amuse yourself?

AGNETHA: Sometimes I wonder if I ever get away from it. I have two small children that seem to take all my time. In whatever's left of my sparetime, I read and listen to music.

FRIDA: I travel as much as I can and try to avoid places where we are well known. I also read a lot.

BJÖRN: I read English and American poetry. I spend a lot of my time at sea, at my house in the Stockholm Archipelago and with my children.

BENNY: I also spend a lot of time at sea - I'm a boat freak. Otherwise, I'm very sporty. I sometimes go so far as to play chess with the window open....We have a life outside of showbusiness; an important life that we always try to safeguard. It's a question of sometimes forgetting that you're sitting in the spotlight or in front of a camera and simply feel as if you're sharing a good meal with your best friends.

A transcript of the conversation between Dick Cavett and ABBA.

Benny performed the Andersson/Ulvaeus composition "Lottis schottis" – still unreleased at the time – on accordion during the taping of the TV special. Unfortunately, this segment was not included in the final version of the show.

BJÖRN ULVÆUS
ANNI-FRID/FRIDA/LYNGSTAD
AGNETHA FÄLTSKOG
BENNY ANDERSSON

The prominent talk show host Dick Cavett had been flown in from the United States to interview ABBA.

129

The concert part of the **Dick Cavett Meets ABBA** special featured the performance of nine ABBA songs, two of which ("Two For The Price Of One" and "Slipping Through My Fingers") were taken from ABBA's as yet unreleased **The Visitors** album.

You look better on the photograph if you laugh

PICTURES FOR THE 1982 OFFICIAL ABBA CALENDAR *spring and summer 1981*

THROUGHOUT ABBA'S CAREER there was a constant demand for new pictures to be published in the press the world over. At the end of 1977 an official ABBA magazine was started in England, appropriately called *ABBA Magazine* (at the end of 1981 it changed its name to *International ABBA Magazine*). It naturally had a high demand for pictures.

The production company behind the magazine also put together a calendar every year from 1981 to 1984, with the calendars for 1982 and 1983 consisting solely of Anders Hanser's pictures. The photo shoots often had to be done very quickly, and Anders mostly looked up the ABBA members at home or at other places where they happened to be. For example, when he visited the Polar studio to take some calendar pictures of Björn and Benny in May 1981, they were working on tracks for the forthcoming album *The Visitors*.

When he was "on location" with the ABBA members, Anders mostly used his 35mm Nikon cameras, shooting slides as well as black and white pictures. It was only when he photographed the group in his own studio, and had a little more time to work with composition and lighting, that he sometimes used his Hasselblad camera. Even then he usually worked alone, with no assistants or make-up people present most of the time. Anders Hanser's assignment in some ways mirrored that of video director Lasse Hallström: producing a great number of pictures in the shortest time possible, using his imagination to come up with ways of accomplishing a sense of variety in the photographs.

Working out different poses for the pictures was mostly a collaboration between himself and the ABBA members, and it was something of a relief for everybody concerned when they did not have to take the assignment too seriously. One example is the series of pictures featuring Frida pulling an amazing range of funny faces, which were published in the 1982 calendar.

Neither you nor
I'm to blame

WHEN ALL IS SAID AND DONE *making of video, 29th August, 1981*

WHILE RECORDING THE *The Visitors* album, ABBA found it hard to come up with a suitable single release. As early as the spring there was talk about trying to issue a single as soon as possible, but it was only in December 1981, when the whole album was completed and already available in the shops, that the first single, "One Of Us", was released.

During the summer of 1981 there was probably a tentative plan to release "When All Is Said And Done" as the first single, for on 29th August a video by Lasse Hallström was taped. The scenes featuring Frida walking on a rocky outcrop were shot on an island in the Stockholm archipelago. "We flew out to the outer archipelago in a helicopter, filmed for an hour or so, and then flew back again", remembers Lasse. The rest of the video was then made in the studio of film production company Filmbolaget in Solna, just north of Stockholm, with exterior scenes being shot in nearby streets.

However, it was only at the end of 1981 that the song became a single, and then only in a few selected countries such as the United States, where it was released as the first single off the current album. By that time, the video had already received its world première in the TV special *Dick Cavett Meets ABBA*, broadcast in Sweden in September.

On 12th February, 1981, the front pages of the Swedish evening papers declared that Frida and Benny of ABBA were to get a divorce. In an instant, the last vestiges of the image of ABBA as a group where the love between the members was completely intertwined with the making of the music were finally erased. Friendship and mutual respect were the concepts that set the tone for future collaboration within the group.

ONLY A FEW DAYS BEFORE the announcement of the divorce, Björn and Benny had started writing songs for what was to become ABBA's *The Visitors* album, and in mid-March the first songs were recorded. For Björn as lyricist, it had become increasingly important to write lyrics that felt personally and emotionally authentic. To produce words that sounded good when they were sung, but didn't really have any meaning beyond the song itself – which was not a problem for ABBA during the first half of their career – was not an interesting challenge for him anymore.

The lyrics for "When All Is Said And Done" are an excellent example of this new approach, for Björn's words were to a large degree coloured by the divorce between Frida and Benny. Björn was a little wary of revealing anything too private in a song lyric, but for Frida there was no doubt that the sentiments expressed touched her deeply. "All my sadness was captured in that song", she has acknowledged.

Frida during the taping of the "When All Is Said And Done" video. Lasse Hallström: "When Frida mimed her vocals, I played the tape at double speed so that her hair moved in slow motion when you played the video back at the correct speed. I made many experiments like that."

One of us
is crying

ONE OF US *making of video, 23rd November, 1981*

ITS ORIGINAL WORKING TITLE BEING "Nummer 1" ("Number 1"), it was perhaps inevitable that "One Of Us" would become one of the hottest contenders for a first single release from ABBA's 1981 recording sessions.

Together with other tracks from the album, in mid-November the song was sent out to the group's record companies all over the world, as final decisions were made over the first single. While Benny and Stig were less certain about "One Of Us", Björn really believed in the song – as did most of the record company representatives they'd approached – and so it did become the first track to be released in seven-inch format.

On 23rd November, a video directed by Lasse Hallström was made. As was the case with "Happy New Year" in the autumn of 1980, some scenes were filmed in Hallström's apartment, where Agnetha acted the part of a woman who had just moved into a new flat. Other sequences were shot at the studios of Filmbolaget in Solna.

Agnetha and Lasse Hallström during the making of the video for "One Of Us" at Hallström's apartment.

In the "One Of Us" video, Agnetha acted the part of a woman moving in to a new apartment.

"One Of Us" was yet another of the songs featuring a divorce theme that, although certainly a prominent lyrical thread for ABBA since the mid-1970s, had grown to primarily colour the last few albums. By way of contrast, the overall upbeat arrangement of the song still made it an easily accessible pop song – it became ABBA's last truly great hit single – that was not particularly representative of the *The Visitors* LP as a whole.

ABBA at the studios of Filmbolaget. During the making of the "One Of Us" video, Lasse Hallström experimented with mirror effects.

Indeed, the rest of the album was quite a melancholy product, featuring lyrics dealing with everything from Soviet Union dissidents (the title track) to the fear of an impending war ("Soldiers"). Other songs simply mirrored the fact that all four ABBA members had now become grown-ups, for instance "Slipping Through My Fingers", where the lyrics were a reflection on Björn's and Agnetha's daughter Linda.

AS FOR FUTURE CREATIVE inclinations on the part of Björn and Benny, perhaps the musical-flavoured "I Let The Music Speak" pointed to a frustration that was making itself increasingly felt in their songwriting process: The team of Andersson / Ulvaeus were getting eager to express themselves musically outside the three-minute pop song format.

The whole conception of the album was marked by a certain gloom, and was something of an uphill struggle. The fact that the group now consisted of two divorced couples sometimes made for a strained atmosphere. However, with all four members being true professionals and still united in their love for creating music, they found both the strength and the motivation to continue working within the group format.

She's a girl with a taste for the world

HEAD OVER HEELS *making of video, 21st January, 1982*

AS A FOLLOW-UP TO THE "ONE OF US" **SINGLE,** most countries chose to release "Head Over Heels", taken from *The Visitors*. However, the song became one of ABBA's least successful singles since their breakthrough. Part of the reason for this failure was perhaps to be found in the conflict between the slightly amusing story in the lyrics, dealing with a trendy woman rushing through life, and the cold sound of the actual recording. Quite simply, "Head Over Heels" was meant to be a tongue-in-cheek, uplifting pop song in the vein of "Mamma Mia" or "When I Kissed The Teacher", but, as Björn later put it, "didn't quite get there".

Perhaps the record buying public was also starting to lose interest in ABBA – an ABBA single would no longer become a hit as a matter of course when the tone for current pop music was suddenly set by New Romantic and synth groups like Duran Duran and The Human League. Björn has acknowledged that ABBA were starting to get slightly out of sync with the world of pop music around this time.

"Head Over Heels" was the last video Lasse Hallström ever did for ABBA, the exterior scenes being shot in central Stockholm on 21st January, 1982. The interior sequences were filmed the same day in the studios of the film company Svensk Filmindustri. Even if the song did not become a success as a single, the video was fairly amusing, featuring Frida as the woman on the go and Björn as her "constantly tired" husband.

Concludes Lasse Hallström of his years as ABBA's video director: "It was a pleasure to be allowed to work with them. I have always liked their music, but at the time working with them was frowned upon a bit in certain circles. That's why I think it's wonderful that they have been vindicated: the music still holds up well. It was damned good back then, and it's still great today."

In the "Head Over Heels" video, Frida acted the part of a woman on the go, while Björn was her husband: "constantly tired", as the lyrics would have it.

The "Head Over Heels" video featured Frida in a variety of dresses. The gold lamé ensemble came from Remis.

Frida put this dress on back to front, so that the deep back became a décolletage.

The top was made by the Japanese designer Kansaï.

A lace dress from Phillippe Salvet.

This dress was designed by Frida's friend Lillebil Ankarcrona.

The chintz dress was made by designer Christine Bergselje.

This pantsuit was bought in Paris.

IN HINDSIGHT, IT'S QUITE CLEAR that 1982 was a transitional year for ABBA. The group slowed down on their activities and gradually all but faded away, while the individual members started looking towards extracurricular projects. For her part, Frida decided to spend the early part of the year recording a solo album. The idea had come to her in the summer of 1981, and was reinforced by the knowledge that Björn and Benny intended to spend time with the newborn babies their wives were both expecting at the start of the new year. "We knew that after we had finished ABBA's *The Visitors* album we wouldn't have much on the agenda", Frida explained. "Since I am a workaholic and always need to have something to do, I decided I'd do a solo album."

It was also during the summer of 1981, while spending time at her country house, that she discovered Genesis drummer Phil Collins' first solo album, *Face Value*, which had been released earlier that same year. "My daughter brought along a tape with different songs on it. One of them was called 'In The Air Tonight' [the first hit single off the album], and it sounded more fresh than anything I'd heard for a very long time", said Frida. "A while later I bought the album at a gas station near my place in the country and played it every single day for eight months."

Collins' album was coloured by a divorce he had recently gone through, and Frida, newly divorced from Benny, was hit straight in the heart by *Face Value*. "When it was decided that I would be recording my own solo album, Phil was the only producer I could imagine working with", she said.

Frida visited Phil Collins at Genesis' studio in England, where she explained how much his album had meant to her and asked him to produce her album. Collins said yes, and the recording sessions for what was to become the album *Something's Going On* took place at Polar Music Studios between 15th February and 31st March, 1982.

When ABBA were recording, Frida and Agnetha would as a rule come to the studio only when it was time to record the vocals. In this case, Frida wanted to be a part of the project all the way through, and accordingly she was present for every single day of recording. "We have literally lived in the studio for two months. We have only had one weekend off", said Frida.

Before the sessions started, Frida spent Christmas 1981 in Austria, reportedly going through 500 songs. After listening to further contributions from specially invited composers, she ultimately picked eleven suitable songs. The compositions came from all sides of the music business. Most of the material had never been recorded previously, but the song "To Turn The Stone" was culled from an unreleased Donna Summer album.

Although Frida stated that the music was more important than the lyrics on this particular album, there was at least one song where the words meant a lot to her. "Threnody" was a poem by American critic, author and poet Dorothy Parker, for which the music was written by Swedish singer Per Gessle, later to find worldwide fame as one half of Roxette. "If I should do an album that is a bit different one day, it would consist of Dorothy Parker poems set to music", explained Frida. "It is from her work that I get strength, insight and comfort when I go through difficult times. Her books have meant a lot to me."

Phil Collins did not have time to write anything new for the project, so Frida recorded "You Know What I Mean", one of the more poignant "divorce" tracks on the *Face Value* album. Björn and Benny were trying to write a song for the album, but by the end of the sessions, they still hadn't come up with anything suitable. Frida stated that if they did, the song would still be recorded for inclusion on the album, but this ultimately didn't happen.

DURING THE ABBA YEARS, when Frida was asked which her favourite artists were, she would often mention soul and funk acts like Stevie Wonder, Rufus, and Earth Wind & Fire. With a few exceptions, this seldom left its mark on ABBA's music in any obvious way. However, the soul factor was to colour some of the tracks on *Something's Going On*, perhaps most obviously the ballad "Baby Don't You Cry No More" which featured the horn section of Earth Wind & Fire.

It could be argued that the sound and singing style that Frida had used on the ABBA's "The Visitors", recorded just a few months earlier, also set the tone for the album in certain respects, in combination with the drum-based Phil Collins sound – "heavier stuff than we usually record in the group", as Frida herself put it. "It's something new and different. It's not pop, not new wave, not rock. A little bit unusual and with a character all of its own."

Frida was the first ABBA member in almost seven years to release a solo album, and of course she was well aware of the high expectations resting on her shoulders after the success of the past decade. However, she seemed to have a realistic view of the situation: "My ambition has been to do the best I can with the material we have chosen, and if that isn't good enough there isn't much I can do about it. All I know is that I have paid attention to every single detail."

The slightly experimental tone of the album, and its departure from the ABBA sound that had made Frida famous, caused some concern at Polar. Phil Collins later remembered that while they listened through the album for the first time at the home of Stig Anderson, the latter remarked: "Ah, there are no singles!"

Although it was true that the album was hardly packed with hit material, the first single, "I Know There's Something Going On", became a sizeable hit, reaching number 13 on the US charts, and selling 3 million copies worldwide.

Producer Phil Collins with Frida, preparing a vocal performance.

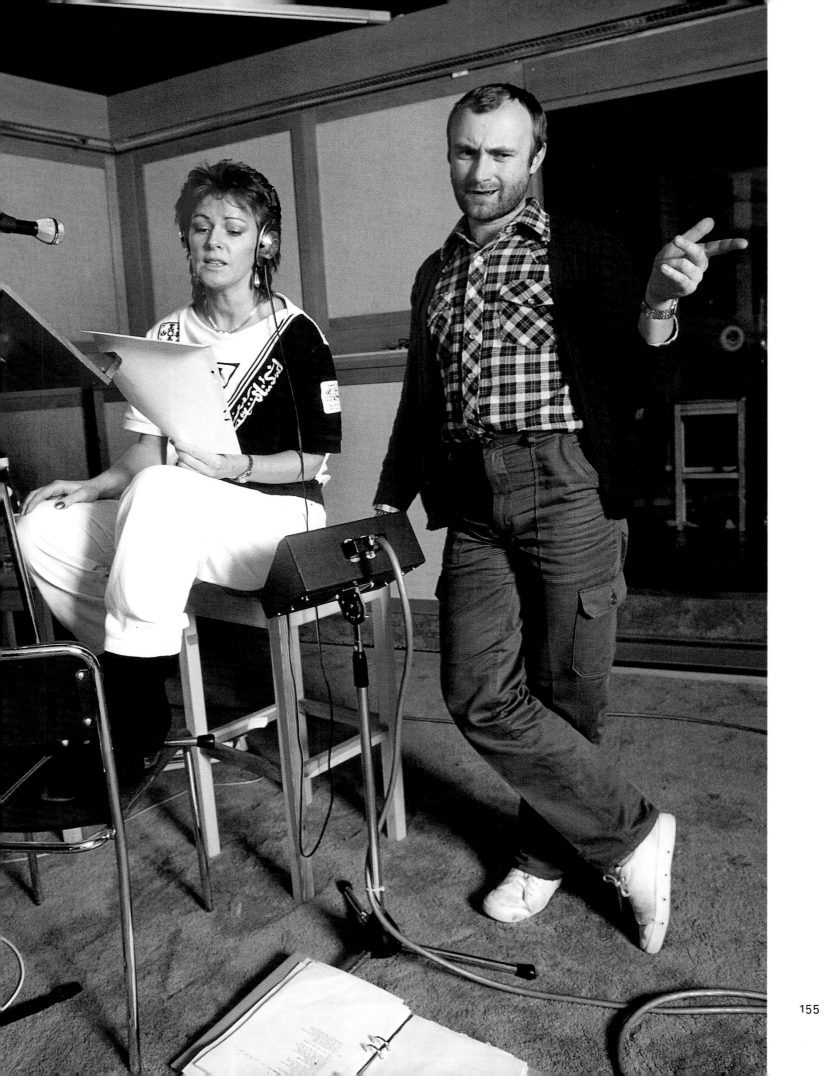

The press conference launching the album, 29th March, 1982.

Frida and Phil Collins with keyboardist Peter Robinson during the sessions for the **Something's Going On** album.

Frida, Phil Collins, sound engineers Paris Edvinsson (back row, left) and Hugh Padgham (far right) together with the musicians on the album.

Something's Going On was released in September 1982, entering the Swedish charts at Number One, and selling more than 1 million copies worldwide.

Anders Hanser is probably the photographer who has taken the greatest number of pictures of the ABBA members through the years, but he never took a picture for the sleeve of any of their official albums.

A picture from Anders Hanser's photo session with Frida was used by artist Yves Poyet when he created the illustration for Frida's album cover.

"I am not that kind of photographer. What I like is to tell a story with a series of different photographs, and to capture fleeting moments. There were others that were better at nailing that one brilliant-looking, 'arty' shot that you needed for an album cover", Anders explains. However, his pictures often ended up on inner sleeves and on covers of singles and compilation albums.

He was also co-creator of the cover for Frida's solo album. Even if his photograph did not adorn the actual cover, the drawing by artist Yves Poyet was made from a picture he had taken. "One of Frida's friends knew this artist, and Frida asked me to take a photo that he could use to paint a picture of." The original picture, taken in Anders' studio in Stockholm, was used on the inner sleeve.

Although the final title of the album had become *Something's Going On* – named after the first single "I Know There's Something Going On" – one early idea had been to name the album after the track "I See Red". The press release issued in conjunction with the album hinted at some of the reasons behind this, describing "the colourful personality of Frida Lyngstad: Red, as in 'I See Red', where red is the colour of love and warmth, temperament and involvement, and where red is Frida."

Some of this thinking seems to have informed the finished album packaging, especially the pictures Anders Hanser took of Frida, which, using her hair as basis, had a glowing red tint all over them. Frida herself said about the title she finally chose: "I thought it was a good title, because something *is* going on. From the moment I began working on this album, I felt some kind of development starting inside me."

In the spring of 1983, Frida made a video for the single release "Here We'll Stay", taken from the **Something's Going On** album.

Frida recording vocals for the **Something's Going On** album.

Look at me standing here again

ABBA at Anders Hanser's Stockholm photo studio, 30th March, 1982. This picture was later used for the sleeve of the single "The Day Before You Came".

PICTURES FOR THE 1983 OFFICIAL ABBA CALENDAR *March–May 1982*

ANOTHER YEAR, ANOTHER CALENDAR – another series of photo sessions. The cover picture for the 1983 calendar is probably one of the most widespread ABBA photographs ever, for the next decade it was to adorn the back of the cover for the 1992 compilation *ABBA Gold*. Before this CD was released in the spring of 1999 – with a different picture – around 13 million copies had been sold worldwide.

This picture was created for the cover of the 1983 ABBA calendar, and later appeared on the sleeve of the **ABBA Gold** album. The group was photographed holding a black sheet over a piece of cardboard. The ABBA logo was then inserted into the picture.

Frida and Agnetha –
the voices that made
the ABBA sound.

Benny listening to a playback of ABBA's latest recordings, which also turned out to be their very last.

Now the last
day is dawning

THE FINAL ABBA RECORDING SESSIONS *Polar Music Studios, August 1982*

AT THE START OF 1982, ABBA's plans for the year were to go on working within the same format as usual: songwriting periods followed by recording sessions, ultimately resulting in a brand new album of fresh material. At one point there was even talk of putting together a double album, with one LP being studio-recorded and the other taped at a specially arranged concert at some venue in Europe.

In the end, however, these elaborate plans came to nothing, and shortly after ABBA had finished their first 1982 recording sessions in June, the decision was made to release the double album *The Singles – The First Ten Years* instead. This new hits package would contain singles from 1973 up to the present, plus two new songs. The group did not feel great about any of the songs recorded thus far, however, and it was only in August that they produced two recordings that could be included on the album as well as being released as single A-sides.

These sessions in August turned out to be the very last for the group, and yielded a total of three recordings: "Under Attack", "Cassandra" and "The Day Before You Came". "Under Attack" became the A-side of ABBA's final single, while "The Day Before You Came" and "Cassandra" were the A- and B-sides respectively of the first ABBA single to be released in the autumn.

Michael Tretow has pointed out that there was a definite sense of closure in the studio when "The Day Before You Came",

Björn, Benny and Michael Tretow working on the latest recordings. Left: Michael Tretow with the digital recorders at the Polar Music Studios.

the last ABBA song ever to be recorded, was committed to tape. Indeed, although the ABBA members themselves stated at the time that they believed there'd be a continued career for the group, in hindsight it seems fairly clear that they had an underlying feeling of the end of an era approaching.

I must have left my house at eight, because I always do

THE DAY BEFORE YOU CAME *making of video, 21st September, 1982*

THE VERY LAST SONG ABBA RECORDED was "The Day Before You Came", which became the first of two singles released during the autumn. The song was written in the studio, and with its stripped-down arrangement it became a miniature melodrama which pointed towards the musical style that would characterise the next stage of Björn and Benny's career.

On 21st September a video was made for the song, filmed in locations such as the commuter train station of Tumba (south of Stockholm), the multistorey car park at Arlanda Airport and the China Theatre in Stockholm. First-time

ABBA video producers were the team of director Kjell Sundvall and cinematographer Kjell-Åke Andersson, who had received a great deal of attention with a couple of their TV movies.

It was Björn who called the team up and asked them if they wanted to direct the videos for two ABBA songs. The idea came from his wife Lena, who was working in the advertising business and had done a commercial with Sundvall and Andersson.

"We nearly fell off our chairs when Björn rang; we'd never done anything like that before", remembers Kjell-Åke Andersson. "They sent us the songs and they wanted a suggestion for them fairly soon afterwards. We went out to Björn's house, talked through our ideas, and then we set to work. Of course, it was terribly exciting and something really special, because ABBA were still very huge."

However, Kjell Sundvall remembers their excitement being a bit clouded: "I had been a part of the progressive left-wing movement during the 1970s and had been criticising ABBA. We were a bit ashamed to be working with them, because it wasn't exactly a cool thing to do in those circles. I tried to make sure that not too many people knew that I had done ABBA videos."

Since the lyrics of the song had a very clear story – a woman listing all the dull, ordinary things she did the day before she had some kind of life-changing encounter with a man – it was quite easy to come up with a storyline for the

The scenes featuring the whole group in the video for "The Day Before You Came" were filmed at the China Theatre in Stockholm.

ABBA with Björn's and Agnetha's son Christian.

Cinematographer Kjell-Åke Andersson (left) and director Kjell Sundvall (right) working with ABBA on the video for "The Day Before You Came".

video. Agnetha was the lead vocalist on the recording, and accordingly acted the part of the woman in the song. Additional scenes featuring the whole group – which didn't really have anything to do with the rest of the storyline – were filmed at the China Theatre, since all of ABBA had to be visible in the video somehow.

Shooting went smoothly – "Agnetha was incredibly easy to work with", remembers Kjell-Åke Andersson – although there was a heart-stopping moment when some of the aerial shots were filmed. "There is a kind of cool helicopter shot when the train passes over the Årstabron bridge, but when we filmed it I almost fell out", recalls Andersson. "I was strapped, but you sort of hang outside the helicopter when you film scenes like that. All of a sudden the pilot made a 180 degree turn, and there is plenty of force when you do that, so it was kind of scary."

"The Day Before You Came" was released as a single on 20th October, but did not become the global success that was normally expected from an ABBA single. Above all, it was a bit worrying that the single did not manage to climb higher than number 32 on the singles chart in the UK, usually the first country to invent and adapt to new musical trends.

At the same time, the double album *The Singles – The First Ten Years* reached Number One on the album chart. A summary of ABBA's past career was apparently more attractive to the pop audience than the new adventures in music that Björn and Benny sought out. Björn later confirmed that they all felt that ABBA's old spark simply wasn't there anymore. "The energy had run out", he said. "That's the feeling we had at the time."

Nevertheless, "The Day Before You Came" as a song and a recording must rank as one of ABBA's masterpieces and a more than worthy swansong, even if it did lack the immediate catchiness that the record-buying public expected from the group. Although it was perhaps too early to dismiss the foursome concept completely, it was definitely time for a break.

Look this way,
just a little smile, is what they say

ABBA at The Dorchester Hotel, London, rehearsing their television performance.

PROMOTIONAL VISIT TO LONDON *5th–7th November, 1982*

THE COMPILATION DOUBLE ALBUM *The Singles – The First Ten Years* was released in the UK on 5th November, 1982. Interest in their new musical direction was limited, but ABBA as pop icons retained a magic aura, and they went to London for a promotional visit to celebrate their ten years together as a group.

Along with a number of interviews with press and radio, two television appearances were made: Agnetha and Benny answered viewers' questions in a live phone-in on *Saturday Superstore*, and later the same day the whole group were guests on *The Late Late Breakfast Show*, where they were interviewed and performed a live version of "Thank You For The Music".

More important in terms of ABBA's future was Björn and Benny's meeting with lyricist Tim Rice. They'd had their first encounter in Stockholm in December 1981, discussing a possible collaboration on a musical, but it was only at the London meeting, almost a year later, that they finally decided to go ahead with the project.

ABBA with host Noel Edmonds, rehearsing their appearance on **The Late Late Breakfast Show** (bottom), and performing a live version of "Thank You For The Music" during the actual broadcast (top).

However, for the moment, the only decision that had been made was that they would actually write a musical – when or under what circumstances was still unresolved. Indeed, as yet Björn and Benny still intended to start writing songs for a brand new ABBA album in January 1983, which left the pair with the dilemma of trying to figure out a way of developing the musical in parallel with the album project. As they soon would realise, this was simply not a realistic prospect.

Benny and Agnetha appeared on **Saturday Superstore** and answered questions during a live phone-in.

ABBA meet the press and celebrate their first and, as it turned out, last ten years together. On 5th November, press receptions were held at The Dorchester Hotel and The Belfry Club.

Agnetha with Mike Chapman, who had agreed to produce her upcoming solo album.

TV personality Kenny Everett with Anders Hanser. In the background: Björn and CBS record company boss Maurice Oberstein. Photo by Benny Andersson.

175

About to crack, defences breaking

UNDER ATTACK *making of video, 16th November, 1982*

THE VERY LAST SINGLE to be conceived and released by ABBA was "Under Attack", recorded around the same time as "The Day Before You Came". In November, a video was made in a warehouse in Norra Hammarbyhamnen in Stockholm. Like the clip for "The Day Before You Came", this final video was made by the team of Kjell Sundvall and Kjell-Åke Andersson.

"We both thought it was difficult to come up with a story for that video", says Kjell-Åke Andersson. "I think the title simply gave us the idea that we should go for some kind of thriller atmosphere, and that's why we ended up in that warehouse."

In retrospect, the video somehow seems to send out pretty obvious signals that the ABBA era was drawing to its close. Only a few years earlier the group had been dressed in typically outrageous, colourful ABBA costumes. Now, they appeared in "sensible", sombre clothes, looking like "proper" grown-ups rather than a glitzy pop group. The video even ended with the four of them walking away in the distance, seemingly leaving the ABBA period behind them and opening up a new chapter in their lives. Kjell Sundvall recalls: "It didn't really feel like we had been working with a group, but with four individuals."

Here is where the story ends, this is goodbye

NÖJESMASKINEN *Swedish TV show, 19th November, 1982*

THE LATE LATE BREAKFAST SHOW *UK TV show, 11th December, 1982*

AS PART OF THEIR TEN YEAR celebrations, ABBA participated in a live broadcast of the popular entertainment show *Nöjesmaskinen* on 19th November, 1982. It was the last time the group members appeared on Swedish television together while the group still existed.

It is tempting to theorise that it was the subconscious feeling that the group were about to break up that allowed ABBA to relax and do one of their best TV appearances ever. The four members were very protective about their private lives. Few artists have become so enormously popular and still been able to keep so many details about the ups and downs behind the scenes secret.

The downside of this guarding of their privacy was that the group sometimes came across as a little distanced and slightly anonymous. Perhaps yet another barrier was raised when they were interviewed by foreign media and had to express themselves in a language which was not their mother tongue.

In *Nöjesmaskinen* they were allowed to speak Swedish, and through their easy-going style of conversation, hosts Stina Lundberg and Sven Melander managed to get the group members to be personal without being too confessional, and thus attract sympathy for themselves as individuals.

Journalists and reviewers did indeed note that ABBA appeared more relaxed and witty than usual, and Frida herself observed about the show in a radio interview a few days later: "I think we were very nice. It's good to be able to show the world that we are mature people: four strong individuals who have the courage to stand up for who we are. Of course, this has to do with everything that has happened in our private lives, which has affected our attitudes towards life and made us stronger." Björn simply noted: "You can't do anything else than just be yourself. And we are always witty."

In the show, ABBA relayed everything from interesting observations regarding their career, to reflections on how men and women may react differently when they split up from each other. They also did a playback performance of "Under Attack" as well as a live version of "Thank You For The Music".

ABBA's very last television appearance as a group came on 11th December, 1982 when they were interviewed and performed "Under Attack" and "I Have A Dream" via live Eurovision link-up from Stockholm to the UK TV show *The Late Late Breakfast Show*.

This last-ever collective ABBA interview was hardly monumental, with host Noel Edmonds subjecting the four members to fairly silly questions like "Agnetha, what is the worst holiday you've had?" and "Which was your best Christmas, Benny?". Still, the UK TV audience got to learn that Björn's favourite animal was the moose since it was tall and handsome just like him, and that the most boring film Frida had ever seen was *Gå på vattnet om du kan* ("Walk On Water If You Can"), the Swedish 1979 movie she herself had a small part in.

Frida and Agnetha captured during ABBA's very last photo session.

ABBA are interviewed and perform "I Have A Dream" on **The Late Late Breakfast Show**, their last ever television appearance.

Agnetha, producer Mike Chapman and engineer Michael Tretow during the making of the **Wrap Your Arms Around Me** album.

Temperature is rising to fever pitch

WRAP YOUR ARMS AROUND ME *17th January–end of March 1983*

AGNETHA FÄLTSKOG – THE HEAT IS ON *making of TV special, 17th–18th April, 1983*

WHILE THE FUTURE FOR ABBA as a group remained undecided, Agnetha followed in Frida's footsteps and devoted the beginning of 1983 to recording a solo album: her sixth altogether, but the first in English.

Mike Chapman, who together with songwriting and producing partner Nicky Chinn had enjoyed success during the first half of the 1970s with groups such as The Sweet, Mud and Smokie, had during recent years primarily devoted himself to production work only. His greatest successes had come with groups such as Blondie and The Knack, and he was now chosen as producer for Agnetha's new album.

Work on selecting songs was started during the autumn of 1982, but just like Frida, Agnetha found it difficult to find the right songs. "I have listened through a whole box of tapes without finding one single song that I like, but perhaps my demands are too high", she said.

On 17th January, 1983, recording sessions started at Polar Music Studios. Agnetha did not try to hide the fact that it felt good to do something on her own again: "Making a solo album is something I've been thinking about for several years. It's always fun to do something that is your own thing completely, and there is no getting away from the fact that when you are working within a group, you inevitably have to make compromises."

The British group Smokie helped out with the backing vocals.

Michael Tretow engineered the sessions and remembers working with Chapman as a pleasant experience. "The only problem was that everything took so long. He was funny that way, because he wanted everything to be so cool. The musicians would say, 'Can't we start playing now?' and he would answer, 'No, take it easy, play some pinball, cool down…' It took forever. It seemed like the album would never be finished. It was obvious he was used to working at a different pace."

TIME MANAGEMENT ASIDE, DURING THE *Wrap Your Arms Around Me* sessions, Michael noted that Mike Chapman thoroughly enjoyed working with Agnetha. "He was really on fire and thought it was so much fun. He was so proud to get the chance to work with her. It was like a dream come true, the pinnacle of his career."

Certainly, Chapman was well aware of being the first producer to work with Agnetha after Björn and Benny and the extraordinary success of ABBA: "One of the nice things about doing a solo project, for both Frida and Agnetha, is that they were both able to take the curls out of their hair, let their hair fall down, and say, 'Right, let's just do this any way we want.' There are no preconceived ideas about how Agnetha Fältskog should sound."

Despite Agnetha's obvious talents as songwriter – she had written ten of the eleven songs on her most recent solo album – her only writing contribution to the *Wrap Your Arms Around Me* album was the track "Man". Even then, it took her two months just to come up with this one song. "I am enormously self-critical, which means that most of my compositions are thrown in the wastepaper basket", she said. "It was awfully hard work writing this one song, and I got stuck many times. But I am satisfied with the end result."

Just as Frida had done during sessions for *Something's Going On*, Agnetha took the opportunity to participate in all aspects of the recording of her own album. "I was there from the beginning when the backing tracks were recorded. I sang along, so that the guys would get a picture of the song by hearing the melody. And then, of course, you contribute a few ideas here and there – but without taking over the producer's job."

Also like Frida, Agnetha found that she had to invite composers to submit material when the hundreds of tapes she had gone through did not yield enough good songs. She even approached some of the same composers, including Tomas Ledin, who had written "I Got Something" for Frida and now contributed the reggae-flavoured "Take Good Care Of Your Children". "I like reggae", said Agnetha. "I said to Tomas, 'If you're going to write something, write a reggae song'."

The finished album, *Wrap Your Arms Around Me*, was released on 31st May, 1983, with the title track being Mike Chapman's contribution to the project as composer. Although the album did not become a huge international success, only two days after release it had sold 100,000 copies in Sweden alone, and naturally entered the charts at Number One. The first single off the album, "The Heat Is On", was also the biggest hit, and Agnetha later named it as her favourite from *Wrap Your Arms Around Me*.

On Chapman's suggestion, "The Heat Is On", as well as several other tracks on the album, featured backing vocals from his old protegès Smokie. The group was also present when Agnetha recorded a TV special to promote the album.

Agnetha Fältskog – The Heat Is On was taped on 17th and 18th April, 1983 at the Studion club in Stockholm. The show featured Agnetha performing six songs from the album ("The Heat Is On", "Can't Shake Loose", "Wrap Your Arms Around Me", "I Wish Tonight Could Last Forever", "Mr. Persuasion" and "Shame"), and became an export success for Swedish Television.

One problem that was to dog Agnetha throughout her international solo career was the foreign record companies' attempts to present her simply as "Agnetha" on album covers, her last name Fältskog being thought too difficult to pronounce. In fact, a cover for *Wrap Your Arms Around Me* was produced featuring the name Agnetha only, but that concept did not last very long.

Agnetha during the making of her TV special **Agnetha Fältskog – The Heat Is On**. Berit Andersson, Maritza Horn, Diana Nuñez and Smokie provided backing vocals.

"I didn't feel happy", said Agnetha. "I told them that I just didn't care if they had a problem pronouncing the name. This was important, and I am really happy that I put my foot down. 'Agnetha' could be anybody, but Agnetha Fältskog is only me."

At the time, Agnetha said that she wasn't trying to convey any specific message with her album, but simply wanted to produce enjoyable, upbeat pop music, perhaps as a reaction against the melancholy songs which had been her main repertoire with ABBA over the past few years. "We wanted good songs

Agnetha performed the songs from her new album for the very first time in the TV special **The Heat Is On**.

with strong melodies, a positive spirit. Not just tragic ballads about someone having left you, or that life is difficult."

The whole packaging of the album, featuring Agnetha as a seductress rather than the sad-eyed, lonely woman of latter-day ABBA myth, seemed to suggest that she wanted to project a completely new image that could co-exist with her part as a fourth of ABBA. Indeed, at the time of the album's release she envisioned a future where the group would be the central part of her career, with the solo work and a career in film running parallel.

As it turned out, there was to be no further work with ABBA, and although Agnetha has been offered many, film roles over the years, apart from her appearance in the Swedish 1983 movie *Raskenstam*, none of them has seemed to her to be right.

What remained was her solo career in music, which to date has yielded only two further international albums: *Eyes Of A Woman* in 1985 and *I Stand Alone* in 1987. However, she has stated that of her English language solo albums, it is *Wrap Your Arms Around Me* that remains closest to her heart.

Agnetha – solo in the 1980s.

We are here to sell you chess

CHESS, WRITING AND RECORDING OF CONCEPT ALBUM
January 1983–28th September, 1984
CHESS IN CONCERT TOUR *27th October–1st November, 1984*
CHESS – MUSICAL PREMIÈRE *London, 14th May, 1986*
CHESS – BROADWAY PREMIÈRE *New York, 28th April, 1988*

ASKED AT THE END OF 1976 how he and Benny would go about reinventing themselves and their music, Björn replied: "I guess you would have to involve other media than records, and perhaps try to create something with a wider scope. You have to go for things you have never done, that are new to yourself. It's so important that you get motivation, that you feel that it's inspiring to sink your teeth into something new and not just write ten new songs."

It would be another six years before Björn and Benny finally got the opportunity to put together something with that "wider scope", and when it finally happened it was the realisation of a dream they had had for more than a decade.

During the ABBA years, several attempts were made to get a musical project off the ground, but generally nothing really came of it. The first effort to be made public was the mini-musical *The Girl With The Golden Hair*. It was written for the tour of Europe and Australia in 1977, where it was included as a 20-minute segment during the concerts.

At the end of that year, Polar announced that Björn and Benny were to devote 1978 to writing a complete musical, but those plans were abandoned, and the ABBA album *Voulez-Vous* was recorded instead.

During ABBA's promotional trip to London in November 1982, Björn, Benny and Tim Rice decided to go ahead with their **Chess** project. The trio toasted to celebrate their decision.

When the pair went on a songwriting trip to Barbados in early 1980 they got the idea of writing a musical that would take place on a New Year's Eve. In Barbados they met comedian John Cleese and asked him if he wanted to write the book, but unfortunately he declined. The only result of this idea was the song "Happy New Year" which ended up on the *Super Trouper* album.

Björn and Benny with Tim Rice and Judy Craymer at the Polar building in Stockholm, planning the upcoming **Chess** recording sessions, October 1983. Judy Craymer would later go on to co-produce the **Mamma Mia!** musical with Björn and Benny.

Another idea put forward and then discarded during these years was to write something based on Lewis Carroll's *Alice In Wonderland*.

For several years then, it was a fairly realistic possibility for Björn and Benny to devote time to a musical instead of doing yet another ABBA album. The main reason that it took so many years to achieve was obviously that the demand for ABBA music remained so high during this period. There was also much left to achieve within the framework of the group as a music-making unit.

IT WAS ONLY WHEN ABBA started running out of energy, coinciding with a fading interest in the group from the general public, that Björn and Benny finally made a serious attempt at writing a musical. By that time, they'd also realised that they needed a working partner to write the story, and the task fell to Englishman Tim Rice. American theatre producer Richard Vos provided the connection between the three.

Tim Rice had spent some time developing an idea for a musical about chess as a metaphor for a love story. He was also interested in commenting on the East-West relationship during the Cold War years. Explained Rice: "The lives of great chess players have always been exciting and dramatic. I was captivated by chess during the 1972 world championships in Reykjavik between Boris Spassky and Bobby Fischer. After that, the ideas started taking shape."

By 1980, he had put together a five-page synopsis, partly based on Russian chess player Viktor Kortjnoj's defection to the West in 1976. He showed his story to composer Andrew Lloyd Webber, with whom he'd achieved worldwide fame writing musicals such as *Jesus Christ Superstar* and *Evita*. By that time, however, Lloyd Webber was hard at work on the musical *Cats*, and didn't have time to get involved with Rice's chess concept.

Unable to find any other composers who liked the idea, the disheartened Rice mentioned his struggles to Richard Vos, who had heard from Shelley Schulz of International Creative Management – the company that handled ABBA's affairs in the United States – that Björn and Benny were interested in writing a musical. Perhaps they would be suitable collaborators, suggested Vos.

Tim Rice immediately fell for the idea. "Although creating number one hits is not the same as writing a modern theatrical score, strangely I had no doubts", he later remembered. "There is a sense of theatre in the ABBA style."

IN DECEMBER 1981, Björn, Benny and Tim Rice had their first meeting in Stockholm. "We admired Tim Rice tremendously, and Tim for his part had loved ABBA for several years", remembered Björn. "So he came over, we had dinner at a restaurant and we just instantly clicked." Rice put forward a few different ideas, one of which was centred around Cuba and Fidel Castro. The one Björn and Benny fell for, however, was the chess concept. "We decided to develop the idea", Rice recalled. "I was to hold off talking to other potential composers."

While the elaborate plans for new ABBA recordings during 1982 were slowly but surely whittled down to just a few new songs, Björn's and Benny's inclination to actually go ahead with the musical project – or "rock opera", as they referred to it at the time – grew stronger. A longtime fan of classical music, Benny even started preparing himself musically by listening to operas.

"I want to get a grasp on how they are structured now that we will perhaps collaborate on an opera together with Tim Rice", he said. "Listening to Wagner's *The Mastersingers of Nuremberg* can be an enormous kick." The framework of musicals like *Evita* suggested that Rice shared Björn and Benny's ambition to cut down on the dialogue as much as possible and let the story be told through music and lyrics.

When ABBA visited London in November 1982, Björn and Benny had another meeting with Tim Rice, and finally decided to go ahead with the project. They also decided that they should start by recording a concept album of the musical – as Tim Rice and Andrew Lloyd Webber had done with *Jesus Christ Superstar* and *Evita* – rather than premièring the musical on the stage.

This was a working method that suited the Andersson / Ulvaeus team just fine, as Benny later explained: "We wanted to have a grip on the whole project. We are very familiar with the recording studio, so we wanted to hear it all first before it ended up on stage."

In January, Björn and Benny started writing songs in the attic studio at the Polar offices in Stockholm. The idea was that, using Tim Rice's synopsis as a starting point, they would know roughly what was required at any given point in the plot. Involved from an early stage was arranger and orchestrator Anders Eljas, making his first major contribution to a Björn and Benny project.

Benny, Anders Eljas and Per Lindvall rehearsing the **Chess** score at Benny's attic studio in the Polar building. Benny brought along his young son Ludvig.

Having already impressed the two composers with his "surprise" string arrangement for the "Thank You For The Music" encore in Australia, as well as his arrangements for the *Voulez-Vous* album, Anders had also done some work with the men's choir Mansläpparna ("The Male Lips"), of which Björn and Benny were members. It was a choir put together just for fun which used to perform at birthday parties and other similar functions, and Anders sometimes stepped in as arranger.

Once Björn and Benny had decided to write *Chess*, they asked the prominent pianist Janos Solyom for advice on how to proceed, and which orchestra to use. Solyom said that they should work with the London Symphony Orchestra, and since they had come to realise that Anders Eljas was a very talented arranger they asked him if he wanted to arrange *Chess* for them. Anders had never done anything on that scale before, and was slightly taken aback at first.

"I went home and thought it over, but then I figured, 'What the hell, if you reach for the stars I guess you will at least end up somewhere in between.' So I said yes, and started thinking of how to go about it, studying different scores, asking my old music teachers for advice, and so on."

Michael Tretow, who engineered the demo sessions as well as the final album sessions, remembers the composing period as the piecing together of a gigantic jigsaw puzzle. "Everything is based on the flow of music which comes from Benny", he says. "Much of *Chess* was just their feeling their way through it, as it were. They would have some basic ideas, and then come up with something brilliant that turned out to lead into one of those other pieces."

With Björn writing dummy lyrics as usual, the songs were then committed to tape and sent over to Tim Rice, who wrote proper lyrics for them. Even so, many of Björn's original ideas were left in the final lyrics.

"He used to give me lyrics which were meant to be nonsense lyrics, but they always had wonderful lines in them, which I was able to nick and save myself many hours of pain", remembered Rice. The most famous example was the line "One night in Bangkok makes a hard man humble" from the song "One Night In Bangkok". "I have been told by so many people that this was a complete summary of my brilliance – but Björn wrote it!"

During the songwriting period, a great number of tryout recording sessions were made, when the melodies were sung by singers who could give Björn, Benny and Tim an idea of how the songs sounded when they were sung. For instance, Agnetha recorded a demo song called "Every Good Man", which ended up as "Heaven Help My Heart" in the completed musical, and singers like Tommy Körberg and Björn Skifs, who were both later chosen to appear on the finished album, also helped out.

AT THE END OF JANUARY 1983, Björn, Benny and Tim Rice visited Moscow in order to get some grasp of the atmosphere and cultural environment of the place where a few of the major characters had their roots. In that respect, Moscow would play a significant part in their musical. As it turned out, although a good time was had by all, the trip did not really give them much in terms of creative input. However, they did meet up with Russian singing star Alla Pugachova, who was briefly considered for the role of Svetlana. Ultimately, though, the part went to Barbara Dickson.

Recording work proper for the musical was started on 1 November, 1983 and was at this point scheduled to be completed by the end of May 1984, with the album slated for release in the late summer.

Anders Eljas was given tapes with the music and was told to come up with suitable arrangements. He found the diversity of music styles in *Chess* to be a great help in that respect. "It's such a mix of music, with pastiches of many different styles. I could draw on a certain type of music and then try to do an arrangement in that vein."

Later in November it was also announced that the part of The Russian (Anatoly) would be sung by Tommy Körberg, one of Sweden's finest singers. British musical star Elaine Paige, who had triumphed as *Evita* in London's West End, would play the part of Florence, the American player's second who falls in love with Anatoly.

Recording of backing tracks for the **Chess** score, Polar Music Studios, late 1983. Opposite page: Benny with Anders Eljas (top), Lasse Wellander and Rutger Gunnarsson (bottom). This page: Björn in the control room (top), drummer Per Lindvall (centre).

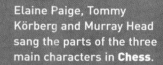

Elaine Paige, Tommy
Körberg and Murray Head
sang the parts of the three
main characters in **Chess**.

Tommy Körberg had of course been among the singers singing on the early *Chess* demos, and could only conclude that "Benny must have been pleased with the result." Indeed he was. "As far as Björn and I are concerned, Tommy Körberg is the best singer imaginable for this part", said Benny. He was equally flattering regarding the talents of Elaine Paige: "She has been my favourite for many years. No other singer has even been considered for this part."

THE PAST HISTORY OF Tommy Körberg and his relationship with Björn and Benny was interesting. During the 1970s, when the Swedish music business was divided into two separate camps – the left-wing so-called progressive movement which insisted that music must have a politically correct message and not be packaged as anything remotely glitzy, and the "pure entertainment" field where ABBA were placed whether they liked it or not – the outspoken Körberg made no secret of his dislike of ABBA and everything they stood for.

"Benny and I had a discussion about this in the 1970s", he recalls today. "I maintained that all this 'lightweight music' got in the way of 'real music'. Benny just replied coolly: 'You are singing the wrong kind of stuff. One day I am going to show you how you should use your voice'." Tommy Körberg's showstopper in *Chess* turned out to be the majestic "Anthem", a song that has almost come to be more associated with him as a performer than the musical as such.

Not long after Körberg and Paige were brought on board, the other major roles were cast as well. The American chess player was to be played by Murray Head, who appeared on the original *Jesus Christ Superstar* concept album. Barbara Dickson, who starred in the musical *Blood Brothers* at the time, got the part of Svetlana, Anatoly's wife.

As Michael Tretow points out, the singers certainly represented different personalities, temperaments, and vocal styles, with everyone making their special contribution to the sessions. Michael's own favourite was Murray Head. "He was so cool! Completely insane and just a bundle of nerves, and with such an expression in his voice that it just sent thrills down your spine."

It had been decided that no expense would be spared in getting the best musicians for the project, and so a session at CTS Studios in London with the London Symphony Orchestra and The Ambrosian Singers was booked for the first week in April 1984. In preparation for this recording, a weekend in late March was spent at the concert hall Berwaldhallen in Stockholm, trying out the string arrangements with pupils from the Royal University College of Music.

"Björn and Benny don't read music, so they had no way of knowing how all these arrangements would sound", remembers Anders Eljas. "Benny has said many times that this was his happiest day during the whole *Chess* project, when he finally got to hear it: 'So *this* is what it's going to sound like. It's going to be great!'"

WHEN THE CHESS TEAM went to the London studio for the proper recording, they also brought with them the core gang of Swedish top session musicians featured on the album: drummer Per Lindvall, guitarist Lasse Wellander and bassist Rutger Gunnarsson – much to the surprise of the English engineers.

"They said, 'Why are you bringing musicians from Sweden?' They felt it was like carrying coals to Newcastle", remembers Michael Tretow. "But then, when the guys started playing 'Bangkok' in those complex cross rhythms, the engineers couldn't believe their ears. Of course, these were the best musicians we had in Sweden, but I implied that this was the standard of the average Swedish musician. It was wonderful to see their jaws drop."

As work on the project progressed, the album's release date was pushed back to October. Björn, Benny and Michael Tretow still had to work around the clock to meet the deadline.

Despite all the hard work, there was no doubt that those involved thoroughly enjoyed the experience. Said Benny after the album had been released: "I have never felt such satisfaction with any work I have done. I was pleased with much of ABBA's music as well, but *Chess* is so much more in terms of atmosphere and substance."

Tommy Körberg and Elaine Paige rehearsing their vocal parts with Björn, Benny and Tim Rice.

Barbara Dickson sang the part of Svetlana.

Denis Quilley sang the part of Molokov on the **Chess** album.

Chess In Concert: Benny played the accordion during the opening number, "Merano".

"We are here to sell you chess."
Björn, Benny and Tim Rice sang a few lines from "Opening Ceremony" at the start of the performance.

On 28th September, 1984, the last mixing session for the concept album was completed. Although enough material had been recorded to fill a triple album, it was felt that it was too hard to market such an expensive product, and the decision was made to release a double album instead.

Ironically, this was on the eve of the explosion of the compact disc format, and a double CD would easily have been able to contain all the recorded work. Sadly, although compact discs had been introduced two years earlier – indeed, *Chess* was released on CD almost simultaneously with the double-LP package – the vinyl album was still dominating the music business, which is why an album's worth of original recordings remains unreleased.

Several of those unused songs and pieces of music have cropped up in stage versions and In Concert performances, however. Yet titles such as "Der Kleine Franz", "Interview" and "Press Conference" indicate that, in all likelihood, no potential hit singles were deleted from the *Chess* score.

No sooner had the album been completed before preparations began for a series of concert performances of *Chess* songs, set up to launch the album. It was a major production featuring no fewer than 250 people, including the London Symphony Orchestra, and was so expensive that sponsorship was required.

On 27th October, the first concert was held at the Barbican Centre in London, and the production continued to Paris, Amsterdam and Hamburg before finishing in Stockholm at Berwaldhallen on 1st November.

The concerts all went smoothly except for this very last one in Stockholm, although the mishap that occurred meant that backing singer Karin Glenmark

really got the chance to shine. Karin had performed the part of Svetlana during all previous concerts on the tour, but for this performance Barbara Dickson, who sang the part on the concept album, was going to appear. The concert was taped for television and it was considered a very special occasion.

However, when the concert was nearing the end, Barbara Dickson felt that she would not be able to reach the high notes in the song "Endgame", and decided to let Karin Glenmark sing instead. Standing among the other backing vocalists, Karin soon realised what was about to happen. "At first I thought Barbara was going to make a late entrance", she recalled, "but when the orchestra had played the first line of the vocal part I realised she was not going to appear. And I realised that the whole number rested on my shoulders." Karin started singing – "Tommy and she ended up having this duet 20 metres apart", says Anders Eljas – and emerged the heroine of the final concert performance.

Apart from this little incident, the tour was a hugely successful enterprise that had been seen through "with little loss of baggage and no loss of inspiration",

Anders Eljas conducting the London Symphony Orchestra.

Karin Glenmark saved the Stockholm performance of **Chess In Concert** when she took over from Barbara Dickson, who failed to appear on stage.

as Tim Rice later put it. All concerned had reason to be equally pleased with the concept album, which had been released on 29th October to mostly rave reviews.

"For me it's the pinnacle of Björn and Benny's career. I don't think I have ever heard music as good as this", says Michael Tretow. "We were working forever on it, and when it was over I still wasn't tired of the songs, and this has never happened to me before. I have heard a lot of music over the years and been tired of a lot of music, but this was just too advanced for an ordinary geek to grow tired of it! Even to this day when I hear it, I enjoy it just as much as I did back then."

The *Chess* album spent seven weeks at the top of the Swedish chart, and reached the UK Top Ten. Two of the single releases from the album were huge hits, with the Elaine Paige and Barbara Dickson duet "I Know Him So Well" spending four weeks at Number One in the UK, and reportedly outselling each and every one of ABBA's UK singles. Similarly, Murray Head's "One Night In Bangkok" – which was by far the biggest international *Chess* hit, reaching number three on the US chart – is in fact said to be the biggest-selling single ever for Björn and Benny, all their ABBA hits included.

Murray Head interpreting the part of The American.

Elaine Paige, Tommy Körberg and
Denis Quilley on stage during the
Chess In Concert tour.

The double album ended up selling two million copies worldwide, which is an extraordinarily good figure for an album from a musical. Tim Rice certainly had reason to be pleased with the way this first project with his new collaborators had turned out:

"There's an enormous difference between writing for theatre and writing pop albums – and both are equally difficult. But in the whole rock era since the 1950s I can't think of any other musicians who have done both with success. The great pop album people couldn't do the musical theatre and I don't think the great theatre writers like Sondheim or, indeed, Andrew [Lloyd Webber] could write an ABBA album. Benny and Björn look as if they can do both."

Chess had unquestionably proved to be a success on the strength of its music and lyrics alone. The next step would be to prove that it worked on stage as well. Originally it was hoped that the première could take place in the autumn of 1985. At one point there was talk of having the opening on Broadway, since the London theatres that would be suitable were occupied by long-running hits.

In April 1985 it was announced that Michael Bennett, famous for musicals such as *A Chorus Line* and *Dream Girls*, would be the director of *Chess*. By that time, Björn, Benny and Tim had definitely decided that they wanted the production to take place in London after all, which led to some disagreement with Bennett and Bernie Jacobs, head of The Shubert Organisation, who were to produce the musical.

Jacobs and Bennett insisted that the musical should open on Broadway. "I was not at all happy about that", said Tim Rice later. "The economics of Broadway are even more extreme than London, and the New York theatre is going through an unhealthy phase. The 'butchers', the newspaper critics there, exert so much power that they can kill shows before the public ever has a chance to make its choice."

Thus, the decision was made to open the show in London, and soon enough the première date of 14th May, 1986 had been set. In the autumn of 1985, the first of what turned out to be almost 1,300 auditions began at the Prince of Wales and Lyric theatres in London. The only definite cast decision was Elaine Paige in the role of Florence, who noted that this was the first time she had participated in the recording of a musical concept album before actually playing the part on stage. "But there are a lot of new songs in addition to the material on the record, so the whole thing is fresh again. It's like approaching a brand new piece almost."

Although it was hoped that both Tommy Körberg and Murray Head would be able to repeat their parts on the record on stage, the writing team and the director considered other actors as well. In truth, they always wanted the three stars of the concept album to appear in the stage version, and as far as Murray Head was concerned, there was little contest.

For Tommy Körberg, however, there were possible difficulties with getting a work permit, since he was not a UK citizen. Also, the unions did have some influence on the casting of Körberg, preferring to give the job to a British actor, although they would have to prove that there was one available that could do the part just as well as Körberg. "So far, none of those who have tried for the part has even been close to Tommy, so I am pretty optimistic", said Benny. It did not take long to establish that Tommy Körberg was the only realistic choice for the part.

Two proud composers shortly before the **Chess** premiére.

Meanwhile, the trio of Björn, Benny and Tim Rice commuted between preparations in London and Stockholm, where they were working on the last details of the book.

In January 1986, disaster struck when it was announced, less than four months before the première, that Michael Bennett had to withdraw from the production because of health problems. Of course, rumours started immediately that Bennett had in fact pulled out because of artistic clashes with Björn, Benny and Tim Rice, or because he was not getting along with Elaine Paige. The truth was that Michael Bennett was seriously ill, and he died of an AIDS-related disease a year later.

The problem with who was going to take over direction had to be solved immediately. At the end of January 1986 it was announced that British director Trevor Nunn of the Royal Shakespeare Company had taken over the production. Nunn had actually been the trio's first choice, but due to a crammed schedule he had been forced to turn down the offer.

As luck would have it, one of Nunn's prior commitments as director had been postponed, which meant that he now would be able to step into the *Chess* production after all. However, as he made clear from the start, Trevor Nunn would put his own slant on the show, and many of the elaborate parts of the set that Michael Bennett had commissioned – including six hydraulic lifts – were rendered redundant. Still, several of the extravagant set pieces conceived by designer Robin Wagner, such as a video-wall consisting of 128 monitors, were left in the show.

The change of director and the ensuing adjustments meant that the rehearsal period had to be shortened. The already tightened production schedule was further reduced by another problem. All the technical gadgetry was causing major headaches, which meant that rehearsals at the Prince Edward Theatre had to be postponed again and again. Small wonder that an exasparated Björn was heard to sigh: "No one in his right mind would undertake a thing like this."

The stars of **Chess**, Siobhán McCarthy, Tommy Körberg, Elaine Paige and Murray Head, on the opening night.

As if the technical problems were not enough, Tommy Körberg collapsed and had to be taken to hospital just a few hours before the very first preview. Nerves and long rehearsal days had taken their toll, but miraculously Tommy was well enough to go through with the night's performance after all.

The last few weeks of rehearsals and previews had also been marked by a constant shifting back and forth of sections in the musical. Parts were being thrown out one day and reinstated the next, creating much extra work for arranger Anders Eljas.

"It is not like a word processor where you can just delete a paragraph – you also have to change the passages preceding the section you take out in order to have them fit with the part that follows. An arrangement is like a journey from A to Z and if you delete the part between, say, L and P, you want to start the journey all over again, and that can take quite some time."

The last days before the opening on 14th May were focused on restructuring the second act, which for some reason did not work. "We spent many nights trying to analyse what was wrong", said Benny. "We felt that there was an imbalance in the plot, that the human relationships were overshadowed by the more intellectual sub-plots: the actual chess game and the East-West relationship."

This meant very hectic times for Anders Eljas and his team of notators. "It was only decided exactly how the second act should be on the day of the première. The theatre was so small that the foyer was the only place with room enough for writing the notation. So while the audience was watching the first act, we had ten notators on their knees out there – some of them were really old men – rewriting the music for us."

However, despite all these last minute adjustments reviews were mixed, with as many critics praising the show unreservedly as damning it completely. The cast got more unanimously excellent reviews, though, and all in all, *Chess* turned out to be a hit with audiences. The show ran for three years, before finally closing on 8th April, 1989.

BY WAY OF CONTRAST, in the spring of 1988 *Chess* had also had a short stint on Broadway, which turned out to be one of the few major setbacks Björn and Benny have experienced in their careers.

At that time, it was clear that although attempts had been made in London to have the musical focus less on the chess match and the political conflicts and more on the romantic plotline, still more work had to be done in that vein.

While director Trevor Nunn had stepped into the London production too late to be able to substantially alter the structure of the musical, this time around he had the opportunity to truly put his personal stamp on the staging of *Chess*. Michael Bennett's approach, relying on a lot of technology, was now to be replaced by a sharper focus on the human aspects.

Furthermore, playwright Richard Nelson was brought in to provide a new book which it was hoped would tighten up the weak plotline. "There is more flesh and blood in this version", said Benny Andersson. "The musical is more comprehensible."

Tommy Körberg and Elaine Paige played the main characters in **Chess**.

The location was the Imperial Theater on 45th and Broadway. No members of the London cast were part of the Broadway production, and the lead parts of Florence, Anatoly and Freddie were instead played by the relative unknowns Judy Kuhn, David Carroll and Philip Casnoff. However, Anders Eljas repeated his role as orchestrator and arranger.

Along with some explanatory dialogue, a couple of previously unheard numbers had also been added to the production – most notably the poignant "Someone Else's Story" – while the opening scene in Merano had been deleted along with the bureaucrat satire "Embassy Lament".

All this rewriting, adding and subtracting was something that Björn and Benny seemed to take in their stride, having learned their lesson after the London production. "To compromise is absolutely necessary. You can't always get what you want, there are so many different things that influence a musical: audibility, costumes, scenery and so on", said Benny shortly before the Broadway opening.

Björn, Benny and Tommy Körberg being interviewed by Swedish television after the première.

Chess on Broadway. Opening night, 28th April, 1988.

"We've also come to understand that you can't run someone else's department. At the present we have a problem with the stage floor, but now we know that there are others who will take care of that. We don't have to worry."

There were other aspects of the staging to worry about, though, and after each performance during the first week of previews, director and composers sat up until the early hours of the morning working on changes and last-minute touches.

Although preliminary ticket sales were very encouraging, disaster struck after the première on 28th April, when the reviews were published. Frank Rich of the

David Carroll played the part of Anatoly when **Chess** was staged on Broadway.

Philip Casnoff, who played Freddie, with Judy Kuhn, who was Florence.

Benny with Judy Kuhn and director Trevor Nunn.

New York Times – also known as "The Butcher" – judged the show very harshly. Such is the power of critics in the Broadway world that a bad review from an influential writer effectively kills all chances of success.

Further changes to the show were made, but it was too late. After only eight weeks *Chess* had to close, much to the astonishment of those involved in the production. It was felt that the New York production was better than the London version: less spectacular, but with a much clearer story.

The Broadway failure of *Chess* has not stopped it from being consistently performed across the United States by regional theatre groups, and also in other countries. The concert version of the musical has remained popular as well, and in 1994 Tim Rice even remarked that "the best interpretations of the work to date have been in concert". Indeed, in Sweden the *Chess In Concert* concept has become a very successful project on its own terms, and is usually performed with the same core gang of Swedish vocalists.

Some 15 years after the musical was first launched, Björn, Tim and Benny all agree that while they are more than satisfied with the music and lyrics, the problem that has continued to dog *Chess* in all subsequent attempts at staging it is simply that no one has really been able to knock the basic story into shape. However, at the time of writing, the trio are again busy restructuring the musical for a definitive version, based on the original mid-1980s concept. Says Tim Rice: "I keep coming back to *Chess* because it is the musical that won't go away. There seems to be a permanent public interest in it."

Frida at the Arc de Triomphe, Paris.

My fantasy makes me shine

FRIDA'S DEMO SESSIONS *Polar Music Studios, April 1983*

SHINE *Studios de la Grande Armée, Paris, 1st February–31st March, 1984*

AFTER HER SPLIT FROM BENNY in 1981, Frida had devoted much of her time to assessing her situation in life and deciding in which direction she wanted to head, artistically, professionally and personally. One of the conclusions she reached was that she wanted to move abroad, and she left Sweden for London in late 1982.

One of Frida's reasons for leaving the country was that she was tired of the stories about herself and the other ABBA members which appeared in the Swedish gossip press. Agnetha had recently filed lawsuits against gossip weeklies that printed false stories about her, and Frida had also had enough of the speculation regarding alleged new boyfriends since her divorce.

At this point she also intended to record her next album in London at the end of 1983. This made her choice of new home town even more convenient. Frida and Phil Collins had both enjoyed their collaboration on the *Something's Going On* album, and while ABBA were still on hold with an uncertain future, Frida naturally wanted to go on exploring uncharted musical territory with Collins at the helm.

Almost immediately after finishing promotional activities for her own album and ABBA's *The Singles* compilation in late 1982, she started thinking about her next project. Above all, urged on by Phil Collins, she wanted to try to come up with some compositions of her own for the first time.

Frida had actually been writing down some rough ideas for lyrics here and there for the past couple of years, but it was only at the end of 1982 that she bought a keyboard and started trying to come up with some melodies. "You could say that this is what I do during my spare time at the moment", she said.

Frida recorded demos of some of her own songs. Members of her backing band during the sessions, Rendez-Vous, included her son Hans (far left) and Benny's son Peter (second from the right).

Frida during sessions for her **Shine** album at the Studios de la Grande Armée, Paris, spring 1984.

Frida explored the soundscapes of the 1980s together with Steve Lillywhite.

"I would like to write everything myself, but I won't be able to pull that off, so there will also be songs written by others."

Frida hoped to have three of her own songs on the album, and in the spring of 1983, she recorded a few demos at Polar Music Studios. As a backing band she used the group Rendez-Vous. Two of the members were none other than her own son Hans Fredriksson and Benny's son Peter Grönvall.

As 1983 progressed, it became clear that Phil Collins wouldn't have the time to produce another Frida album after all. The past year had seen him hit the very big time with chart-topping hits like "You Can't Hurry Love" and "Against All Odds", and he'd simply become too busy balancing his own career and that of his group Genesis to have much time to work with anyone else.

FRIDA INSTEAD TURNED to Steve Lillywhite, who after productions with acts such as Peter Gabriel, U2, Simple Minds and Big Country had become one of the hottest producers of the 1980s. Lillywhite had established a very typical, bombastic 1980s style, signified by lots of echo and crashing drums. This modern, state-of-the-art sound was something that appealed a great deal to Frida.

The studio chosen for the recording of the new album, titled *Shine* upon its release, was Studios de la Grande Armée in Paris, France. Among the backing crew selected by Steve Lillywhite for the recording sessions were Big Country drummer Mark Brzezicki, while backing vocals were provided by Kirsty Mac-Coll, who was Steve Lillywhite's fiancée as well as a singing star in her own right.

Steve Lillywhite and Frida
at the mixing desk.

By the time the sessions started on 1st February, Frida had come up with a total of ten completed songs of her own, but was far from satisfied with all of them. "I have written one or two songs that perhaps could work. It's terribly hard writing both lyrics and music, and often everything just grinds to a halt", she said.

Ultimately, two of her compositions were recorded in Paris, and one of them, "Don't Do It", was included on the finished album. "That's Tough", a song co-written with her son Hans and Kirsty MacColl, became the B-side of "Shine", the first single release off the album.

The other had mostly been picked from a selection of 600 submitted songs, while Björn and Benny also contributed a brand new composition called

Kirsty MacColl, backing vocalist during the **Shine** sessions, with husband-to-be Steve Lillywhite (left). The **Shine** press conference (right).

"Slowly". The song is special in that it marks the last time to date that either Frida or Agnetha has recorded an original Andersson / Ulvaeus composition.

Shine was released in September 1984 to mixed reviews. There was an ambivalence as to whether Frida's inclination to explore the possibilities of contemporary sounds and styles had paid off in terms of actual musical quality. Either way, Frida herself professed to be very pleased with the album.

"The sound is bolder than on the last album. Steve opened me up as a musician. All of a sudden I have reached sounds and a way of working music-ally that I had no outlet for before – but now I have discovered it."

SADLY, THE SHINE ALBUM failed to do as well as Frida had hoped, and the years following the release of the album saw her shift her priorities. She made a few guest appearances on other people's albums, but eventually reached the decision to officially withdraw from the music business.

In September 1987, she even wrote a letter to her fan club, asking it to shut down:

"I now feel it is the right thing to make it clear to you that my life no longer is music, but that I have chosen to go other ways in order to develop potentials which have always been inside me. My decision not to continue as an artist stands there-fore firmly unchanged."

Over the next few years Frida would mainly use her celebrity status to draw attention to environ-mental issues, otherwise taking what must have been a much-needed break from more than 25 years in show business. Her love for music did not die, however, and given time to firmly establish a life out of the limelight, she eventually returned to the recording studio.

So now we'll go separate ways

Görel Hanser holding up the "Tivedshambo" lyrics for the benefit of the ABBA members.

The 1986 version of ABBA with Görel Hanser.

TIVEDSHAMBO *making of tribute video for Stig Anderson, 16th January, 1986*

IN JANUARY 1986, Stig Anderson was to be the subject of *This Is Your Life* on Swedish TV. The format of the show called for important friends and relations from over the years to show up in the programme. With Stig as the subject of the show, ABBA were among the most obvious guests to appear in the show, their relationship with Stig having proven so mutually beneficial over the years.

However, time constraints and prior commitments meant that it was impossible for all four members to travel down to Malmö in the south of Sweden, from where the show was to be broadcast. The solution was to gather them together in Stockholm on 16th January – two days before the broadcast – and tape a lighthearted video performance of Stig's very first hit "Tivedshambo" ("Hambo From Tived").

It was not as if the four members saw each other regularly anyway. Of course, Björn and Benny were still very much involved in their *Chess* project, but neither Frida nor Björn lived in Sweden, and at the time of the taping Agnetha and Frida had not seen each other in two years.

To date, this remains the very last public performance by the former ABBA members. Since then, the four have only been seen under the same roof when attending birthday celebrations of mutual friends. When Görel Hanser turned 50 in June 1999, they even performed a Swedish birthday song together.

THE LOCATION FOR THE VIDEOTAPING of the tribute to Stig was Benny's studio in the attic of the Polar building in central Stockholm. Apart from the ABBA members, the only people present at this fairly momentous occasion were the camera crew and Görel and Anders Hanser.

The taping didn't take more than an hour, and Frida, who had arrived in Stockholm only a few hours earlier, immediately left for the next plane back to her home in Switzerland.

The close-knit family feeling that had surrounded ABBA and Polar was now definitely a thing of the past, and it wasn't without a certain amount of regret that many of those concerned saw everyone go off on their own separate paths in life.

"There was a tremendous separation anxiety when ABBA broke up, for all of us", says Rune Söderqvist. "Görel and I sometimes talk about it, that it was pretty painful for a while. It's like when you are making a movie, for instance, and you are together for a year, and then everybody goes their separate ways. It feels sort of hopeless."

The taping of "Tivedshambo" would have been the sole contribution to *This Is Your Life* of any ABBA member if it had not been for Tony Kaplan, part of the team behind the show, who persuaded Björn and Benny to appear in person as well. Benny was going to be at a party near Malmö on that night anyway, and Björn was talked into coming down from Stockholm, even though he had planned to go back to England, where he was living at the time.

THE SHOW PROVED to be the last time that ABBA and Stig appeared together as friends in the eyes of the world. Because of a business dispute, the relationship between the group and their former manager was rapidly deteriorating at the time. Soon, it was clear that no agreement could be reached, and the whole affair eventually led to a lawsuit that was settled out of court. To determine who was in the right is not the purpose of this book, but the whole affair certainly was, as Agnetha put it in her autobiography *As I Am*, "a sad and sorry end to a successful collaboration".

Sing my happiness

KLINGA MINA KLOCKOR *summer and autumn 1987*

Benny with Orsa Spelmän. Back row, l-r: Nicke Göthe, Leif Göras and Kalle Moraeus. Front row, l-r: Perra Moraeus, Benny Andersson and Olle Moraeus.

"SOME TIME I AM GOING to do an instrumental album, my own solo album – some day, when I have the time", said Benny Andersson in a 1982 interview, reflecting on a thought that even at that time had been with him for several years. After writing and recording the *Chess* musical, putting it on the London stage, and also producing two albums for brother/sister act Gemini, he finally found the time to realise this project in the autumn of 1987.

Although for the past two decades, Benny had primarily been known as a rock and pop musician and composer, his musical roots could actually be found in Swedish folk music. At the age of six he'd been given his first accordion, and started playing together with his father Gösta and his grandfather Efraim.

Only a few years later, the three Andersson men played at local dances in the Stockholm archipelago under the name Benny's Trio.

To this day, the accordion remains Benny's favourite instrument: "Partly because of its connection to my childhood and the Swedish tradition, but there's also the physical aspect of playing the instrument. I like the fact that you get a little hot when you are playing."

ABBA'S MUSIC COULD be described as a combination of Swedish folk music, American rock'n'roll, classical music and Swedish and European "schlagers", all of which are music genres that are close to Benny's heart. However, even during ABBA's heyday, Benny maintained that it was the music of his earliest roots that gave him the greatest pleasure, and even if he himself played the accordion, it was the traditional fiddler's folk music that he loved the most.

Although the folk music influence was seldom apparent in ABBA's music – the title track of ABBA's 1976 *Arrival* album was perhaps an exception – several attempts were made to turn a Björn and Benny tune from the mid-1970s called "Lottis schottis" ("Lotti's Schottische") into an ABBA song. However, none of them came out the way the composers wanted. It was only when Benny finally recorded his solo album *Klinga mina klockor* ("Ring, My Bells") – almost a decade later – that the song found its natural expression in a simple arrangement for accordion and fiddles.

The fiddles on the album were played by the group Orsa Spelmän, marking the start of what has turned out to be a very fruitful collaboration. Less commonly known is the fact that the link between Benny and Orsa Spelmän was provided by none other than Anders Hanser, who was born in the town of Orsa and knew the group members well.

Benny and Orsa Spelmän rehearsing at the Hansers' cottage in Orsa, August 1987.

At Anders' 40th birthday party in 1985, Orsa Spelmän member Kalle Moraeus and a friend had been invited to perform a couple of songs, representing Anders' Orsa roots. Later during the party, a jam session developed, and Benny, never one to miss a chance to play some folk music, asked if he could join in on his accordion. The answer was a resounding yes.

Afterwards, Benny told Kalle Moraeus that he would like Orsa Spelmän to appear on his album of songs written in the tradition of Swedish folk music. It was not until the spring of 1987 that Benny finally found the time to start working in earnest on his solo album, which at the time had the working title *Min melodi* ("My Melody").

In March, he travelled up to Orsa for his first meeting with Orsa Spelmän. This was also the first time that he played with the group, and it seems that the chemistry was there from the beginning between the folk musicians and the ex-pop star.

In August, Benny went up to the Hansers' cottage in Orsa again to rehearse the songs for the album with Orsa Spelmän. It was in Orsa that Benny found time to write one of the most important pieces on the album.

"One day when the rest of us were out in the Björnparken park with the kids, Benny stayed back, and that's when he wrote the tune for the section with the choir in the 'Klinga mina klockor' suite", recalls Anders Hanser. This melody was also used for the opening track of the album, "Inledningsvisa" ("Introduction Song").

"Klinga mina klockor" was recorded later in the autumn, and became the title track of the album. An 11 minute and 30 seconds suite, it culminated in a section featuring an all-star choir of Swedish female singers. Incidentally, the choir included Frida, making her last appearance on record, to date, together with another ABBA member.

ALL IN ALL, THE KLINGA MINA KLOCKOR album was a forum for Benny to express all the music that was inside him, but which hadn't found a release on ABBA's records or in something like the *Chess* project. Indeed, the album – the first on Benny's own Mono Music label – did not really contain anything that could be labelled hit music, which is why he did not expect any significant sales figures, and initially just pressed 12,000 copies.

Upon release in November 1987, the album became a success, however, reaching the Swedish top ten and eventually selling 160,000 copies, sales figures that the average pop album rarely matches in Sweden.

Two years later, Benny recorded a second solo album in a similar vein – his last to date – called *November 1989*, which also appeared on the album charts. As for Benny and Orsa Spelmän, the *Klinga mina klockor* album was the start of a collaboration that has continued to this day, with the group – and even Kalle Moraeus individually – recording albums for the Mono Music label.

Benny with his wife Mona at her 40th birthday.

Benny also appears frequently with Orsa Spelmän on stage, and on those occasions they often perform the song "Födelsedagsvals till Mona" ("Birthday Waltz For Mona", written for the 40th birthday of Benny's wife in 1983), from the *Klinga mina klockor* album.

Benny recording the "Klinga mina klockor" suite with Anders Eljas, members from the Swedish Radio Symphony Orchestra and the all-star female choir at Berwaldhallen, Stockholm, autumn 1987.

The Swedish all-star female choir performs "Klinga mina klockor", recreating the sound of one of Benny's childhood favourites, the girl choir who'd called themselves Postflickorna ("The Post Girls"). Front row: Frida, Lena Andersson, Anna-Lotta Larsson, Lena Philipsson, Maritza Horn, Pernilla Wahlgren, Mia Lindgren, Siw Malmkvist. Back row: Barbro "Lill-Babs" Svensson, Monica Forsberg, Karin Glenmark, Yvonne Erlandsson, Johanna Lundberg, Eva Dahlgren, Anne-Lie Rydé, Ingela "Pling" Forsman, Diana Nuñez, Monica Svensson and Liza Öhman.

King Carl XVI Gustaf took the stage to thank the performers after the concert.

Frida and Marie Fredriksson of Roxette did a duet on the song "What A Wonderful World".

Frida performing her version of Julian Lennon's "Saltwater".

The all-star choir that performed the song "Änglamark": Tomas Ledin, Barbara Bonney, Frida, Gösta Winbergh, Marie Fredriksson, Kristina Hammarström and Håkan Hagegård.

The world I love is dying

MUSIK PÅ BORGGÅRDEN CONCERT *the Royal Palace of Stockholm, 14th August, 1992*

FRIDA'S DECISION TO LEAVE THE music business in the mid-1980s turned out to have a profound effect on her personal life. She was left with a lot of time to figure out who she really was, explore new paths in life and find a new sense of security within herself.

It was this personal journey that ultimately led her on to the dedication to environmental work that her public persona has primarily been associated with during recent years. The catalyst had come when her attention was caught by an article about acid rain. "I felt that I had to do something, not just sit there apathetically and watch all that's happening", she recalled.

The seeds for Frida's commitment to the environment had been planted at an early age, however. "I was very interested in nature as a child. I spent a lot of time by myself outside and enjoyed that", she explained. Her ecological consciousness got a further boost in the late 1970s when she became a vegetarian. Later on she started studying philosophy and religion, searching for a connection between the different aspects of life.

Frida had arrived at this stage in her life when she got the inclination to do something about the state of the environment. After a while, the rumour about her awakened interest in this issue spread, and she was contacted by the organisation Det naturliga steget ("The Natural Step").

It wasn't long before she was part of the executive group of the organisation, and by 1990 the environmental work had become her new profession, totally dominating her waking hours. She spent four or five days each month in Sweden, and the rest of the work was done with the aid of computer, fax and phone from her home in Switzerland.

1990 was also when she started a group within Det naturliga steget called Artister för miljö ("Artists For The Environment"), whose purpose was to encourage actors and singers to draw attention to environmental issues through concerts and other public appearances.

IN 1992, FRIDA RETURNED TO the recording studio for the first time in almost five years, and recorded a single as part of Artister för miljö. The A-side featured the song "Änglamark", written by Evert Taube, one of Sweden's most famous composers, and was performed by Frida along with opera singer Håkan Hagegård, Marie Fredriksson of Roxette, and Tomas Ledin. On the B-side, Frida sang Julian Lennon's 1991 hit "Saltwater" on her own.

This single was recorded as a promotional release for a very special concert arranged by Artister för miljö, called *Musik på Borggården* ("Music On The Courtyard"). It took place in the courtyard of the Royal Palace of Stockholm, where King Carl XVI Gustaf had given permission for a concert to be held for the first time in history.

This event took place on the evening of 14th August, 1992, featuring actor Max von Sydow as compère and offering entertainment from opera singers, a jazz ensemble and popular music singers. Frida sang "Saltwater" and did a special duet with Marie Fredriksson on the Louis Armstrong hit "What A Wonderful World". She also took part in the all-cast finale performance of "Änglamark".

Afterwards, Frida claimed to be very satisfied with the event, her first concert performance in twelve years. "I was never nervous. On the contrary, it was just fun. During the whole concert I felt that the atmosphere was good both in the audience and among the artists."

However, she also pointed out that this return to the recording studio and to the stage was just a one-off thing. "I would consider singing under circumstances like these, but not otherwise", she said. It would take another four years before Frida finally felt ready to record a complete album again, the 1996 Swedish release *Djupa andetag* ("Deep Breaths").

Marie Fredriksson, King Carl XVI Gustaf and Frida after the concert.

As for her environmental work, she soon found that it was impractical for her to have so much responsibility for Det naturliga steget and Artister för miljö while living in Switzerland. Therefore, she decided to leave those organisations and start her own foundation, Stiftelsen Anni-Frid Lyngstads miljöfond ("The Anni-Frid Lyngstad Environmental Foundation").

The primary aim of the foundation, in the words of Frida herself, "is to promote teaching and research in the environmental field. This includes ecology, the working environment, children's and young people's environments as well as inner and spiritual environments."

One way of achieving this has been to arrange environmental summer camps for children every year since 1994. The foundation also has a scholarship which has been awarded annually since 1993 at the Youth Parliament for the Environment. The prize is given to the school that has achieved the best environmental work during the year.

Although she professes that the love of music remains strong within her – and despite her comeback on the music scene in 1996 – there can be little doubt that it is the work related to environmental issues which remains closest to Frida's heart today.

Our dreams of gold were grand

The village of Duvemåla, which author Vilhelm Moberg used as a starting point for his novels about Swedish emigrants.

KRISTINA FRÅN DUVEMÅLA

Musical Première – Malmö Musikteater, 7th October, 1995

Gothenburg production 1996; Stockholm production 1998–1999

AFTER HAVING WRITTEN CHESS and seeing it staged in various incarnations over the years, Björn and Benny had reached one definite conclusion: If they were ever going to do a musical again, it would have to be based on a truly solid story. After taking a break from everything connected with the musical world after the flop with *Chess* on Broadway in the spring of 1988, the inclination to do something in that field again grew stronger.

But where to find that solid story? Björn and Benny both realised that foreign musical writers often went to the great literature of their respective cultures in order to find a story that could form a basis for a musical drama. One well-known latter-day example is the hugely successful Schönberg/Boublil musical *Les Misérables*, based on Victor Hugo's 19th century novel.

After having toyed with various ideas, by 1990 Björn and Benny had settled on Swedish author Vilhelm Moberg's *Emigrants* suite of novels, dealing with the fate of Swedish emigrants to America in the late 19th century.

Said Benny: "Nothing has moved me as much as those novels. But my first thought was, 'There is no use doing it. Everybody has read the books and seen the movies [in the early 1970s director Jan Troell turned the novels into two highly acclaimed feature films].' Perhaps it's a bit unnecessary – but on the other hand no one has heard the music."

This wasn't the first time that Björn and Benny had found Moberg's novels inspiring them to musical creation, for in 1971 they put a song called "Träskofolket" ("The Clog People") on the B-side of a single they released as a duo. Some 20 years later the time had come to extend the story of "starvation and misery and people who left for the west", as the lyrics had it, to a production of more epic proportions.

"To take the step of moving to the other side of the world, and to know that you will not be able to return, although that's what you long for all the time and you never rid yourself of that feeling – there's a lot of music in that", Björn observed.

Such themes also caught the attention of dramatist and playwright Carl-Johan Seth, who was commissioned to produce a script. "The first thing Carl-Johan said was, 'There'd be no point in trying to put *The Emigrants* on stage – if it wasn't for the music'", said Benny. Along the way Björn and Benny had also concluded that they had to focus the musical on Kristina, one of the main characters, in order to make the project manageable.

Director Lars Rudolfsson giving instructions to the cast during rehearsals.

The first couple of years' work on the musical were very much an uphill struggle, and those involved started doubting that they'd be able to come up with something worthwhile. Part of the problem was their admiration for the novels, and only when they created a scenario for themselves where they imagined that Moberg would be able to okay what they were doing were they able to move forward.

"It took me two years before I realised that there is no way this is going to work unless I dare to say, 'Now this is mine and I do what I want with it!'", recalled Benny. "When you start relying on your own choices you can also start trusting them."

BEFORE THEY HAD GOT THAT FAR, however, Björn and Benny took a break from the project and wrote and produced the pop CD *Shapes* for singer Josefin Nilsson. That album was released in the spring of 1993. Meanwhile, Carl-Johan Seth's script was restructured and cut down, and only then did Björn and Benny start to feel that they had something potentially very good on their hands.

In May 1994, it was announced that the musical was going to be called *Kristina från Duvemåla* ("Kristina From Duvemåla") and that it was going to be staged at Malmö Musikteater (Malmö Music Theatre) in the autumn of 1995. It was also revealed that the task of directing the piece had fallen to Lars Rudolfsson, who had previous experience from the world of music theatre, and also shared the writers' view on how to treat their work on stage. Around the same time, it was announced that American Robin Wagner, who had worked on *Chess*, would do the stage design.

By this time, four years had passed since work on the musical had begun. During all this time only half of the necessary music had been written. Even at an early stage, the sheer magnitude of the project made Björn and Benny realise that they'd have to divide their roles as creators of music and lyrics more clearly than ever before.

Said Benny: "Björn and I have made the music together through the years; there have been two of us, and through discussions we have decided how we want it to be. You can have such discussions to a certain extent, but with *Kristina* that doesn't work. If this music should have any relevance whatsoever it must spring from one single person's feelings. In this case, my feelings."

IN JANUARY 1995 IT WAS REVEALED that the relatively unknown Helen Sjöholm had got the leading part as Kristina. "All of us thought that she was the absolute best", said Benny. "She has so many of the qualities that I think Kristina has: some kind of depth and earnestness and integrity. For me, she is the absolutely perfect Kristina from Duvemåla." Benny having spotted her talents a few years earlier, Helen had actually been involved in the creation of the musical at an earlier stage, lending her vocals to several demo recordings.

Actor Anders Ekborg, who got the part as Karl Oskar, had a string of productions in the world of theatre and film behind him, while Peter Jöback, who was to play Robert, was known primarily from his roles in the musicals *Fame* and *Grease* in Stockholm. Åsa Bergh was to tackle the part of Ulrika, and had previously acted in *The Threepenny Opera* and *West Side Story*.

One advantage of knowing who was going to play the leading parts was that the creators got a more concrete early picture of exactly who'd perform what they were writing. The musical turned out to be a major production, with the total number of actors and musicians approaching 150.

Anders Eljas had been called in as arranger yet again, and found *Kristina från Duvemåla* to be a somewhat different experience to *Chess*. Although the sheer scope of the new musical was wider than *Chess*, it proved to be in many respects an easier task. This was partly because Benny now had modern synthesizer equipment, with which he could record demos featuring all instruments exactly as he wanted them to sound.

"Benny's original demos were so much clearer and more detailed this time", says Anders Eljas, "but the difficulty was transferring his recordings to an

Malmö Musikteater on the night of the very first performance of **Kristina från Duvemåla.**

Helen Sjöholm as Kristina and Anders Ekborg as Karl Oskar with two child actors from the Gothenburg Opera cast.

ordinary arrangement for an orchestra. Sometimes there were just too many things happening at the same time, which meant that it would have required an enormous string section to capture everything that was on the tape. This means that you have to organise it all a bit differently, and it can take quite some time to figure out how to make everything work so that it sounds as close to the demo as possible."

WHEN THE MUSICAL OPENED on 7th October, all the hard work proved to be worthwhile, however, for *Kristina från Duvemåla* turned out to be a major hit. The fairy-tale tone of Moberg's work, which Lars Rudolfsson and dramaturgist Jan Mark had focused on, coupled with Robin Wagner's simple but effective stage design and the colourful costumes by Görel Engstrand, seemed to constitute the perfect framework for Benny's very Swedish and typically "Andersson-flavoured" music with lyrics by Björn which hit exactly the right mood.

Peter Jöback as Robert with Björn's and Agnetha's daughter Linda Ulvaeus, who played the part of Elin in the Cirkus production of **Kristina från Duvemåla** in Stockholm.

For Björn, it had been a great challenge to write the lyrics for *Kristina från Duvemåla*. He had complete trust in Benny's ability to write good music, but he was more unsure of his own contribution. "I felt pretty nervous and desperate in the beginning", he recalled. "But then I read the books over and over again to get his language inside my head, so that there would automatically be something of Moberg in the lyrics I wrote."

Judging by the praise the reviewers gave to *Kristina från Duvemåla*, not least the lyrics, Björn could feel secure in the knowledge that he'd achieved what he set out to do. Even if *Chess* had been received with a certain respect, and admiration for ABBA's music has grown in more recent years, *Kristina från Duvemåla* meant that Björn and Benny, for the first time during their long careers, got the chance to relish a virtual unanimity between critics and audiences.

It seemed everybody who was lucky enough to get a ticket to the sold-out performances in Malmö agreed with the hopeful "greeting" that Björn directed towards Vilhelm Moberg in the programme for the musical: "It would be presumptuous to believe that our Kristina is the same as yours. But I think you can be certain of one thing. We love her just as much as you do."

After two seasons at the Gothenburg Opera in 1996 and 1997, the show finally reached Stockholm in February 1998, where it was performed at Cirkus.

Marianne Mörck was Fina-Kajsa, the comical ingredient of the musical.

One of the reasons that such a prestigious production did not receive its world première in Sweden's capital was that there was no suitable stage available. This problem was solved when it was decided that Cirkus, a listed building with a long, impressive history in Swedish showbusiness, would be rebuilt especially for *Kristina*.

THE STOCKHOLM PRODUCTION turned out to be one of the biggest ever by a Swedish private theatre. However, about a year after the Stockholm première, and after having played to over one million people, ticket sales had started to slow down somewhat, and the last performance came on 19th June, 1999.

Although there was inevitably a sense of regret in the air when the show closed, the statistics for the past few years were impressive enough: 671 performances, one million tickets sold, major breakthroughs for the principal actors – and for Björn and Benny, the pleasure of knowing that they had created what turned out to be a national treasure.

Singers Tommy Körberg, Karin Glenmark, Helen Sjöholm and Anders Glenmark on stage.

A song to sing

B&B CONCERTS *Stockholm, 31st October, 1998 and Beijing and Shanghai, March 1999*

EVER SINCE THE PEAK YEARS OF ABBA'S popularity in the 1970s, a notion has existed – based on the way they were treated by some of the media – that the group was never really as big in Sweden as it was in other countries. Certainly, in several Swedish newspapers, radio shows and television programmes, ABBA were regarded as the commercial "antichrist", their music shallow and blatantly seductive, lacking both substance and relevance.

However, parallel to this, the group was loved by the general public like no other artists before or since, with each and every one of their regular albums reaching Number One on the charts*. Sales figures were also impressive, and ABBA's are among some of the best-selling albums ever in Sweden.

Furthermore, affection for the individual members' solo projects did not dwindle after they went their separate ways. The *Chess* double album topped the charts, as did Frida's *Something's Going On* and *Djupa andetag*, as well as Agnetha's *Wrap Your Arms Around Me* and *I Stand Alone*.

Most of the other post-ABBA albums also featured in the Top Ten, and when the *ABBA Gold* album was released in 1992, it too stormed up the Swedish charts, as it did in many other countries, spending four weeks at Number One. As these statistics show, ABBA were and remain well-loved in their home country, no matter what the critics or anyone else said.

By 1995 and the success of *Kristina från Duvemåla*, there was finally a convergence between the reviewers' opinions and the public's love for the group. Over the years, the working relationship between Björn and Benny – by that time spanning almost 30 years – had also begun to crystallise as a history on its own terms, resulting in a most impressive body of work. That was certainly the conclusion reached by producer Johan Englund, managing director of Swedish concert promoters Nordic Artist.

In the spring of 1996, Nordic Artist had two successful productions behind them, featuring cast members from musicals staged in London and New York respectively. Recalls Englund: "Suddenly it struck me: 'Now we have done two concerts featuring the best of London and New York, but we have two great

* *The 1973 Ring Ring album only reached Number Two on the combined singles and albums sales chart featured in Sweden at the time, but since it was the "Ring Ring" single that stopped it from reaching the top position, the album would have reached Number One if there had been a separate album chart.*

Conductor Anders Eljas, Tommy Körberg, Helen Sjöholm, Benny Andersson, Karin Glenmark and Anders Glenmark after the Stockholm performance.

composers right here in Sweden. Why can't we do a concert with the best of their work?'" At that time his idea was primarily to do songs from the Andersson / Ulvaeus musicals, or songs that were in the more "serious" vein, rather than ABBA's pop songs. "The song 'Klinga mina klockor' was like a symbol for the whole project as far as I was concerned. It's like the essence of everything they-'ve been doing during recent years. At one point the whole concert was even going to be called *Klinga mina klockor*."

Johan Englund let the idea mature for a little over a year before approaching Björn and Benny's representative Görel Hanser. She asked him to send over a list of possible songs to be featured in the concert. In early 1998, Englund sat down with choreographer and director Hans Marklund to come up with a list of their favourite Andersson / Ulvaeus compositions. At their first attempt, they ended up with several pages of songs. "We had to start all over again, and said, 'Let's just list 20 songs each and see how many of those end up being the same'", remembers Englund. "The result was that we got an idea for a show and also some ideas about which performers would be suitable."

It was during these discussions that the realisation dawned on them that they should perhaps include some ABBA songs in the programme. "We thought, 'These songs are almost never performed live, they are damned good, and if we do them in arrangements close to the original recordings, but with a symphony orchestra added, it could work really well.'"

BJÖRN AND BENNY GAVE THE PROJECT their seal of approval, offering suggestions for titles to be included or removed from the programme. "Benny was especially adamant that the ABBA numbers should not be a hits-medley, but that the complete songs should be performed", recalls Johan Englund.

The next step was to have a meeting with the artists to discuss the repertoire. The artists chosen to perform the songs were Tommy Körberg, Helen Sjöholm and Karin and Anders Glenmark, along with Orsa Spelmän, all of whom had been working extensively with Björn and Benny in the past. The orchestra was the prestigious Gothenburg Symphony Orchestra, augmented by the Gothenburg Symphonic Chorus.

"Meeting with the artists was almost like starting all over again, because we put away all our lists of songs and asked them, 'What would *you* like to do?'" says Johan Englund. For instance, when he was first asked to participate in the

concert, Anders Glenmark especially liked the idea of performing ABBA songs. "He said, 'I don't want to do a musical concert. If I am going to be part of this, I want to do ABBA songs. That's what's really fun.'" Indeed, more than half of the concert programme ended up consisting of ABBA titles.

Helen Sjöholm, the latest in a long row of singers who have achieved their breakthrough after performing songs by Björn and Benny.

ANDERS IMMEDIATELY STARTED taking an active part in the song selection, and it was he who suggested that he should do the old Hep Stars hit "Sunny Girl", the only song in the concert to have been written by Benny alone.

Apart from the idea that there should be two sections where all four vocalists performed ABBA songs together, the artists also got to choose one favourite ABBA song of their own, most of them having very clear notions of what they wanted to do.

"Tommy said from the beginning that he wanted to do 'The Winner Takes It All'. Anders was clear about wanting to take on 'Knowing Me, Knowing You', and like the excellent record producer he is, also helped Helen to find her own favourite, which was 'Money, Money, Money'." Karin Glenmark chose what turned out to be a stunning rendition of "My Love, My Life".

Tommy Körberg wanted to do "Guldet blev till sand" ("Gold Can Turn To Sand"), by far the biggest hit from *Kristina från Duvemåla* in the original version by Peter Jöback. "That was really great, because I don't think anyone would've dared suggest that", says Johan Englund.

Anders Glenmark performed several ABBA songs, but also "Pity The Child" from **Chess**.

The ever-present Anders Eljas conducted the orchestra with full force.

Helen Sjöholm's solo performances included ABBA songs as well as selections from **Chess** and **Kristina från Duvemåla**.

Karin Glenmark shone in dramatic ballads such as ABBA's "My Love, My Life" and the movie theme "Mio min Mio".

Tommy Körberg and Kalle Moraeus of Orsa Spelmän during the encore performance of ˝Thank You For The Music˝.

One of the more unusual numbers in the show was Helen Sjöholm's performance of "Dum Dum Diddle", together with the fiddle playing of Orsa Spelmän's Kalle Moraeus. Helen knew from the beginning that she wanted to do something with Orsa Spelmän, but although in retrospect it seems an obvious idea, it took quite some time before the right concept was reached: a duet on this song about a girl, trying to get the attention of a man who is "practising hard, playing night and day" on his violin.

ANDERS ELJAS ALSO PLAYED an invaluable part in the project. Although he didn't have time to do all the arrangements himself, he wrote down suggestions to the arrangers on how to approach them. "I made brief 'sketches' where I wrote things like, 'don't forget to have some woodwind here' and 'this part should preferably be that long'. It was more like a manual, and then it was up to them to actually write the arrangements."

When the concerts were announced – one each for Gothenburg and

Stockholm – tickets soon sold out, and no less than two extra concerts for each city had to be added. The first concerts were held at the Scandinavium in Gothenburg on 19th and 20th September, 1998 in front of an ecstatic audience, and were followed by mostly favourable reviews.

ALL THREE GOTHENBURG CONCERTS were recorded by Benny for release on CD only one month later, a further sign of his growing commitment to the project. "Throughout the development of the concert programme, both Björn and Benny maintained that 'this is your production, this isn't our project', and they really wanted to keep themselves in the background", says Johan Englund. "But then Benny came to the rehearsals in Stockholm, sat down at the piano and helped Tommy find his way into 'Guldet blev till sand'. And then he asked if it was okay to record the Gothenburg concerts and make an album from them."

For the Stockholm concerts, Benny asked that an extra piano be put on stage, just in case he felt like participating. "He didn't want to promise anything, or raise people's expectations, because then you can easily end up in a situation where you can't do the concert without Benny going on stage."

As it was, Benny did indeed feel like being a part of the third and last of the Stockholm concerts – much to the excitement of the audience, who ran up to

the stage, cheering along when he played the piano in the last of the two ABBA sections in the show.

The success with the concerts continued in March 1999 when the whole package went to China for two nights, at the Beijing Exhibitional Hall in Beijing on 5th March and at the Shanghai International Gymnastics Centre in Shanghai on 10th March. Björn was present to introduce the Beijing concert, while Benny did the same for the Shanghai performance.

Originally a part of a cultural and business exchange between Gothenburg and China – titled "Sweden Goes To China" – it was actually the Gothenburg Symphony Orchestra that had been invited to participate, not the *B&B* concerts as such. The original plan was to do a performance of *Chess In Concert*, a production the orchestra was more than familiar with, not least through a 1994 performance that was recorded and released on Benny's Mono Music label.

However, since ABBA's music was and is extremely popular in China, it was thought better to bring over the *B&B* concept. Both Björn and Benny, who had never been in China before, took the opportunity to tag along. Björn found it exciting being in Beijing and visiting places like the Great Wall of China and the Forbidden City.

THE CHINA CONCERTS meant a lot of logistical problems, though, since a lot of items that the Chinese arrangers had vowed to provide simply weren't available when the Swedish team arrived. It was only thanks to the skills of the technicians who were part of the team that the concerts could be held at all.

That said, the China performances were a success, and at the time of writing it is clear that the *B&B* concert will certainly go on as a Swedish and international concept for a while yet, much to the satisfaction of everyone concerned. As Johan Englund concludes: "I felt from the start that it was a great honour to work with this material, and I can honestly say that this is the most enjoyable project I have ever been involved with."

The **B&B** concerts turned out to be one of the most successful concert events of 1998 and 1999 in Sweden.

Although they were not really performing as artists in the **B&B** concerts, both Björn and Benny appeared on stage during the concerts in China.

Cheers from the audience for **B&B** in China.

Benny meets the Chinese media in Shanghai.

Out and about in China.
Top: Benny in Shanghai.
Right: Björn in the
Forbidden City.
Centre: Anders Eljas
in Chinese guise.
Bottom: Orsa Spelmän
on the Great Wall of
China.

How can I resist you?

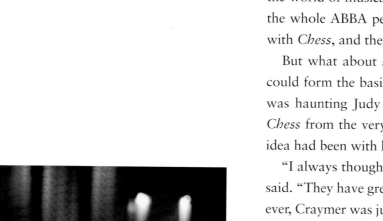

MAMMA MIA! MUSICAL PREMIÈRE *London, 6th April, 1999*

ANYONE WHO STUDIES ABBA'S LYRICS at length will find that many of them are self-contained mini-stories, a description that's especially true of later lyrics like "Our Last Summer" or "The Day Before You Came".

Björn has remarked that "The Day Before You Came" – the very last song ABBA ever recorded – is an example of his and Benny's gradual drift towards the world of musical drama that had been at the back of their minds during the whole ABBA period. The dream of creating a musical finally came true with *Chess*, and then continued with *Kristina från Duvemåla*.

But what about all those old ABBA songs? Was there no way that they could form the basis for a musical of their own? This was the question that was haunting Judy Craymer, heavily involved with the production side of *Chess* from the very beginning, and a good friend of Björn and Benny. The idea had been with her ever since the days of *Chess* in the mid-1980s.

"I always thought there was tremendous potential in the songs", she later said. "They have great emotional tension, and each one has a subtext." However, Craymer was just as aware as anyone else that it would be a difficult task to weave a story around songs which already existed independently.

Björn and Benny, more interested in creating new works than revisiting their past, shrugged their shoulders and said that if she could come up with a suitable idea, they might give the project their blessing. Any involvement from their side would have to be very limited, however.

Over the years, several ideas were brought forward and discarded – at one point it was even going to be a production for television as opposed to a stage musical. Meanwhile, Björn found himself in London's West End with his daughters one night to see the musical *Grease*. That's when he started warming to the idea, and thinking along the lines of creating something that could work as good family entertainment.

"It struck me that an upbeat musical with a good story and lots of hit songs is something very nice to go to see and has great potential. It's the kind of thing I'd like to see myself, and suddenly I saw what could be made with such a musical based on ABBA music."

Björn also decided that he'd like to take a greater part in the project than he had first thought. He saw an opportunity to be a part of the West End theatre world again. "I was longing for a show again, in an almost childish way; to have a show of your own that you could keep your eye on at nights." However, Benny, while supportive, still decided to keep his commitment on a lower level.

Björn and Benny in deep concentration during the final rehearsals for **Mamma Mia!**

Björn and Benny consider the simple but effective **Mamma Mia!** stage design.

In 1996 Björn and Benny went into partnership with Judy Craymer and her co-producer Richard East to form the company Littlestar Services Ltd, which was to produce the projected musical. A little while later, Judy Craymer also found the appropriate writer, playwright Catherine Johnson, who'd won several awards for her work. Johnson's wry sense of humour appealed to Craymer, who thought her perfectly suited to writing the book for an ABBA musical.

In January 1997, the two women had their first meeting, and both agreed from the outset that the musical shouldn't be any wallowing in nostalgia. Indeed, Björn and Benny themselves were adamant that it wouldn't be a tribute show where the songs were simply performed, tied together by a wafer-thin story line.

It was equally, if not more, important that the musical should not be the story of ABBA. Accordingly, Judy Craymer's first instructions to Catherine Johnson contained the key-words "contemporary, ironic, comedy-romance", but left out any reference to ABBA themselves.

A few weeks later, Johnson had completed an outline for a story about a mother and daughter on a holiday resort island, bearing the tentative working title *Summer Night City*. The plot would be centred around the girl having invited three men, all of whom could be her father, to her own wedding.

The ladies who pull the strings: **Mamma Mia!** producer Judy Craymer (left) with Görel Hanser (right), friend and associate of Björn and Benny for more than 30 years.

Björn read the story and liked it: "I realised it was actually possible to use ABBA's original lyrics as a basis for a story about relationships. In the beginning of our career the songs were more innocent and naïve, towards the end they were more mature. And it was women who sang them. Therein lay the opening for a story about a mother and a daughter."

STILL, IT WAS NO EASY TASK for Catherine Johnson to make songs and plot work together, and more specifically, to create a natural flow between dialogue and songs: "We didn't want to have those awful clunky moments where people burst into song", she recalled. "I had to come at it differently – whatever happens in the story, I always have to come back to the song."

By the spring of 1998, the name of the musical had changed to *Mamma Mia!*, and director Phyllida Lloyd, set designer Mark Thompson and choreographer Anthony van Laast had all been brought on board. All through the year work on the musical progressed, resulting in several different drafts of the manuscript.

Siobhán McCarthy on stage.

In September, auditions for the main characters started. Siobhán McCarthy, who had played the role of Svetlana in the original stage production of *Chess*, got the part as Donna, the mother. "I have always loved ABBA and I cried with joy when I got offered the part", she recalled, adding that this was one of the easiest parts she had ever had to learn. "I knew all the songs already. The lyrics are ingrained in me since my youth."

Donna's daughter Sophie was to be played by Norwegian actress Lisa Stokke, while Andrew Langtree got the part as her fiancé Sky. Both Stokke and Langtree were graduates of the Liverpool Institute of Performing Arts, a *Fame*-style school, well-known for receiving support and funds from Paul McCartney.

In October 1998, it was announced that the première would take place on 6th April, 1999, 25 years to the day since ABBA won the Eurovision Song Contest with "Waterloo". Although this seemed to be a clever marketing ploy, Björn insisted that it was pure coincidence. He explained that the date had simply been set to accommodate the schedule of busy director Phyllida Lloyd, who would start work on another production immediately after *Mamma Mia!*

When tickets went on sale in mid-November, it was clear that the show was going to be a huge hit. After only four days, close to £1 million worth of tickets had been sold. This was certainly good news for the show's financial backers, and perhaps such advance success also helped relieve the tension during preparations for the musical. Shortly before rehearsals started, Phyllida Lloyd observed:

"I know that new musicals can be absolute misery to work on, with everyone being absolutely horrible to each other. But so far it's all been very harmonious and I'm optimistic."

REHEARSALS STARTED ON 25th January, 1999, and over the following two months the show slowly came together, with Björn present to oversee proceedings between Monday and Friday virtually every week. Since the opening of *Mamma Mia!* coincided with the 25th anniversary of ABBA's Eurovision Song Contest victory, the spring also saw him conducting innumerable promotional interviews and talk show appearances, primarily in the UK.

Björn and Benny in London's West End, days before the opening of their latest hit show.

Siobhán McCarthy turned in a bravura performance as the character Donna in **Mamma Mia!**

Siobhán McCarthy with Hilton McRae who plays Sam Carmichael, one of the three men who could be Sophie's father.

It's doubtful any of the ABBA members made themselves available to the media to this extent even during the group's most hectic years in the 1970s. Benny – a notoriously reluctant interviewee – said that Björn should be given an award for all the interviews he had done.

On 23rd March the preview period started, and it was clear from the very first performance that *Mamma Mia!* was packed with enough well-known ABBA hits to keep audiences more than satisfied. Also, the two album tracks "Our Last Summer" and "Slipping Through My Fingers" were given a new lease of life by their inclusion in the show.

However, for the sake of the flow of the performance, some sacrifices had already been made along the way. One such casualty was the previously un-released ABBA song "Just Like That", which had been included in rehearsals as a romantic duet between the young lovers Sophie and Sky, but was removed from the show before this first public performance.

BY THE PREMIÈRE ON 6TH APRIL, 1999, the musical had finally gelled into a form that satisfied all involved in the production. Theatregoers and critics alike seemed to agree, with most reviews being very positive, and the audience cheering and singing along to their favourite ABBA songs.

Since then, *Mamma Mia!* has continued playing to capacity houses, and the musical has broken all previous box office records at the Prince Edward Theatre. Furthermore, the year 2000 has seen a Canadian production of the show in Toronto, followed by a tour of the United States.

Louise Plowright in the character of Tanya,
a friend of Donna's who used to perform with her
in the group Donna & The Dynamos in the 1970s.

The cast of **Mamma Mia!** in one of the many lively scenes in the show.

A major factor in the success of the show was that the production team had not fallen into the trap of trying to make ABBA's songs fit into some sort of "message" musical. "No one is pretending to make a serious, epic musical here", said Judy Craymer. "There's a tongue-in-cheek campness about it that is part of the charm we want to retain."

IT'S BEEN SUGGESTED that this tone of campness sometimes becomes slightly odd, as audiences tend to burst into affectionate laughter when a piece of dialogue cleverly leads into the beginning of a well-known hit. In the case of something as charged with painful emotions as "The Winner Takes It All", for example, the show could appear to be selling out the genuine feelings behind this and many other ABBA songs.

One advantage of including relatively unfamiliar titles like "Slipping Through My Fingers" in *Mamma Mia!* was that such songs didn't provoke a reaction of amusement at the start, and proved to be among the most poignant

Donna & The Dynamos in distinctly 1970s-flavoured stage costumes.

Louise Plowright and Paul Clarkson (top), Jenny Galloway and Nicolas Colicos (centre), Siobhán McCarthy and Hilton McRae (bottom).

Björn, Benny and book writer Catherine Johnson greet the audience at the opening of **Mamma Mia!**

Björn and Benny read the **Mamma Mia!** reviews.

Björn and Benny with Lisa Stokke at the opening night party.

The cast of **Mamma Mia!**
in the finale of the show.

Siobhán McCarthy and Lisa Stokke as
mother Donna and daughter Sophie.

moments in the show. The lyrics for "Slipping Through My Fingers" had been written by Björn about his and Agnetha's daughter Linda, and his mixed feelings about seeing her grow up and then away from him. In the show, it was of course Donna who sang the song about Sophie.

However, perhaps the true success of the treatment of the songs lay in a realisation on the part of the musical-makers that most of them had been performed to their full emotional potential by ABBA themselves, and particularly in terms of Agnetha's and Frida's vocal interpretations. There was only one way to go: into semi-light entertainment and the "good night out" that Björn had envisioned.

ALTHOUGH THE MALE HALF of ABBA has come to be respected as a self-contained composer team, irrespective of who actually performs their material, they themselves definitely recognise Agnetha's and Frida's input and importance to ABBA's success. As Benny put it when it turned out that the two singers were unable to attend the *Mamma Mia!* première: "It's a pity that Frida and Agnetha are not here to enjoy the reactions. As it is, Björn and I get all the attention, but without them, none of this would have happened."

Author's acknowledgments

THE TEXT IN THIS BOOK is based on research conducted by me, Carl Magnus Palm, in public and private archives over several years. Out of the many sources used, I would like to mention the following, which have all been particularly useful for quotes: the Swedish newspapers *Aftonbladet, Dagens Nyheter, Expressen* and *Kvällsposten*, the Swedish magazines *Damernas Värld, Mersmak* and *Vecko-Revyn*, the British magazine *Mojo*, the Swedish radio programmes *B för Björn Ulvaeus, Tonträff* and *Kristina från Duvemåla*.

ADDITIONAL INFORMATION has been found in the following books and booklets:

Agnetha Fältskog with Brita Åhman. *As I Am – ABBA Before & Beyond*, Virgin Publishing, London 1997.

Paul Gambaccini, Tim Rice, Jonathan Rice. *British Hit Singles*, GRR Publications Ltd., Enfield 1993.

Eric Hallberg. *Kvällstoppen i P3*, Drift Musik, Värmdö 1993.

William Hartston. *Chess: The Making Of A Musical*, Pavilion Books, London 1986.

Mamma Mia! programme, London 1999.

Organisation Générale des Amateurs d'Eurovision. *A Song For Europe 1956–1998*, Great Britain 1998.

Lars Rudolfsson & Jan Mark. *Bortom en vid ocean – Kristina från Duvemåla*, LeanderMalmsten, Lund 1996.

Wille Wendt. *Topplistan – The Official Swedish Single & Album Charts 1975–1993*, Premium Publishing, Stockholm 1993.

Joel Whitburn. *Top Pop Albums 1955–1996*, Record Research Inc., Menomonee Falls 1996.

Joel Whitburn. *Top Pop Singles 1955–1996*, Record Research Inc., Menomonee Falls 1997.

THE FOLLOWING PEOPLE have contributed valuable information and support, and are warmly thanked: *Hans Barksjö, Sara Barnes, Örjan Blix, Håkan Borg, George Bourdaniotis, Graham Coult, Matthew Crocker, Claes Davidsson, Simon Finn, George Friesen, Kaarin Goodburn, Jeffrey de Hart, Jos Heselmans, Alex Jones, Ian Jones, Noel King, William Meisinger, Gunnar Moe, Trent Nickson, Thomas Nordin, Jean-Marie Potiez, Kristina Radford, Graeme Read, Mike Scurr, Patrick Smith, Ty Turner, Robert Verbeek, Björn Waldenström, Grant Whittingham* and *Jack Wong*. A collective thanks to the members of the Internet mailing list *ABBAMAIL* (www.abbamail.com), where information and opinions flow freely.

The following interviewees are warmly thanked: *Kjell-Åke Andersson, Anders Eljas, Johan Englund, Lasse Hallström, Owe Sandström, Rune Söderqvist* and *Michael B. Tretow*. Grateful thanks also to *Tommy Körberg, Björn Skifs* and *Kjell Sundvall*, who were interviewed by *Anders Hanser*.

At Premium Publishing: Thanks to *Wille Wendt* and *Fredrik Söder*.
At Virgin Publishing: Thanks to *James Bennett* and *Chris Roberts*.

SPECIAL THANKS to *Ian Cole* and *Thomas Winberg* who have both had to grit their teeth through early drafts of my manuscript. They responded by providing facts, encouraging commentary, honest critique and "kill-your-darlings".

GRATEFUL THANKS to *Görel Hanser* for generous assistance.

EXTRA SPECIAL THANKS to *Anders Hanser* for allowing me to put words to your pictures, and to *Agnetha Fältskog, Björn Ulvaeus, Benny Andersson* and *Anni-Frid Lyngstad* for making it all happen.

Official web site, ABBA – The Site: www.abbasite.com

THE LYRIC QUOTES IN THE CHAPTER HEADINGS
were taken from the following songs:

I am your music, I am your song from *Andante, Andante*.
With a bit of rock music, everything is fine from *Dancing Queen*.
The summer air was soft and warm from *Our Last Summer*.
I don't wanna talk about the things we've gone through from *The Winner Takes It All*.
Smiling, having fun, feeling like a number one from *Super Trouper*.
No more champagne, and the fireworks are through from *Happy New Year*.
Hova's witness – full speed ahead from *Hovas vittne*.
Why don't we meet for a chat from *Two For The Price Of One*.
You look better on the photograph if you laugh from *I'm A Marionette*.
Neither you nor I'm to blame from *When All Is Said And Done*.
One of us is crying from *One Of Us*.
She's a girl with a taste for the world from *Head Over Heels*.
I see red from *I See Red*.
Look at me standing here again from *As Good As New*.
Now the last day is dawning from *Cassandra*.
I must have left my house at eight, because I always do f
rom *The Day Before You Came*.
Look this way, just a little smile, is what they say from *I'm A Marionette*.
About to crack, defences breaking from *Under Attack*.
Here is where the story ends, this is goodbye f
rom *Knowing Me, Knowing You*.
Temperature is rising to fever pitch from *The Heat Is On*.
We are here to sell you chess from *Opening Ceremony*.
My fantasy makes me shine from *Shine*.
So now we'll go separate ways from *My Love, My Life*.
The city don't know what the city is getting from *One Night In Bangkok*.
Sing my happiness from *Klinga mina klockor*.
The world I love is dying from *Saltwater*.
Our dreams of gold were grand from *Gold Can Turn To Sand*.
A song to sing from *I Have A Dream*.
How can I resist you? from *Mamma Mia*.

ALL SONGS WRITTEN BY Benny Andersson and Björn Ulvaeus, except *Dancing Queen, Knowing Me, Knowing You, My Love, My Life* and *Mamma Mia* by Benny Andersson, Stig Anderson and Björn Ulvaeus; *Hovas vittne* by Benny Andersson, Björn Ulvaeus, Agnetha Fältskog, Anni-Frid Lyngstad, Michael B. Tretow and Rune Söderqvist; *I See Red* by Jim Rafferty; *The Heat Is On* by Florrie Palmer and Tony Ashton; *Opening Ceremony* and *One Night In Bangkok* by Benny Andersson, Tim Rice and Björn Ulvaeus; *Shine* by Kevin Jarvis, Guy Fletcher and Jeremy Bird; *Saltwater* by Julian Lennon, Leslie Spiro and Markus Spiro.